BUTTERWORTHS ANNOTATED LEGISLATION SERVICE

STATUTES SUPPLEMENT No. 205

THE EUROPEAN COMMUNITIES ACT 1972

By

EDWARD H. WALL, M.A. (Cantab.)
of Lincoln's Inn, Barrister

LONDON
BUTTERWORTHS
1973

ENGLAND: BUTTERWORTH & CO. (PUBLISHERS) LTD.
LONDON: 88 KINGSWAY, WC2B 6AB

AUSTRALIA: BUTTERWORTHS PTY. LTD.
SYDNEY: 586 PACIFIC HIGHWAY, CHATSWOOD, NSW 2067
MELBOURNE: 343 LITTLE COLLINS STREET, 3000
BRISBANE: 240 QUEEN STREET, 4000

CANADA: BUTTERWORTH & CO. (CANADA) LTD.
TORONTO: 14 CURITY AVENUE, 374

NEW ZEALAND: BUTTERWORTHS OF NEW ZEALAND LTD.
WELLINGTON: 26–28 WARING TAYLOR STREET, 1

SOUTH AFRICA: BUTTERWORTH & CO. (SOUTH AFRICA) (PTY.) LTD
DURBAN: 152–154 GALE STREET

ISBN 0 406 54714 9

MADE AND PRINTED IN GREAT BRITAIN BY
BUTLER AND TANNER LTD
FROME AND LONDON

PREFACE

The European Communities Act 1972, in a mere twelve comparatively short sections and four schedules, not only makes general provision for the implementation of Community law in the United Kingdom and, so far as treaty commitments render it necessary, in the Channel Islands, the Isle of Man and Gibraltar, it also makes considerable amendments in eight widely different branches of United Kingdom substantive law, partly in order to remove incompatibilities with Community law and partly in order that new tasks arising from membership of the Communities may be performed.

Though it leaves the bulk of United Kingdom law untouched, the Act contains not only the surprises of novelty, but great potential for effecting further legal change—and a multitude of ramifications to satisfy even the most imaginative explorer. When, therefore, my publishers asked me to prepare a commentary on the Act, my very first steps were to enlist helpers, from a wide range of expertise, and to decide to restrict my commentary to the severely practical.

In preparing this book I have had the great benefit of the valuable and unstinted assistance of a number of persons in Government service, some of whom took part in the preparation of the Bill from the early stages. For their comments and suggestions, many of which are now reflected in the final text of the book, as well as for the kindness with which they proffered them, I am most grateful—and only regret that I am debarred, for obvious reasons, from mentioning them here by name.

I can, however, and do with pleasure, thank the Hon. Kenneth Suenson-Taylor Q.C., who with equal kindness gave me much assistance in regard to the section of the Act concerned with company law.

For the faults and errors in the book I take responsibility alone, as indeed also for the final text of the commentary.

I would also like to express my appreciation of the unfailing courtesy and efficiency of Messrs. Butterworths during the preparation of the book for publication.

E. H. WALL

PREFACE

CONTENTS

PAGE

Preface iii

Table of Cases vii

DIVISION I
INTRODUCTION

PARA.

INTRODUCTION TO THE ACT

The novelty of the original Three Community Treaties 4

Direct and Indirect effects of the Treaties within a member State of the Communities 9

Each Community an autonomous legal order 11

Directly applicable Community Law 16

Construction and Interpretation 23

DIVISION II
THE EUROPEAN COMMUNITIES ACT 1972

Arrangement of sections 28

DIVISION III
SELECTED ORDERS

1. The Intervention Board for Agricultural Produce Order 1972, S.I. 1972 No. 1578 71

2. The European Communities (Enforcement of Community Judgments) Order 1972, S.I. 1972 No. 1590 73

PAGE

Index 107

TABLE OF CASES

PARA.

Attorney-General *v.* Prince Ernest Augustus of Hanover, [1957] A.C. 436; [1957] 1 All E.R. 49; [1957] 2 W.L.R. 1; 101 Sol. Jo. 66, H.L. 25

Boaler, *Re*, [1915] 1 K.B. 21; [1914–15] All E.R. Rep. 1022; 83 L.J.K.B. 1629; 111 L.T. 497; 30 T.L.R. 580; 58 Sol. Jo. 634; 24 Cox C.C. 335; 78 J.P. 280, C.A... 25

Confédération Nationale des Producteurs de Fruits et Légumes *v.* Conseil de la C.E.E., 16–17/62, [1963] C.M.L.R. 160; 8 Recueil 901 22

Costa *v.* E.N.E.L., 6/64, [1964] C.M.L.R. 425; 10 Recueil 1143 .. 18, 19, 21

Ellerman Lines, Ltd. *v.* Murray, [1931] A.C. 126; [1930] All E.R. Rep. 503; 100 L.J.P. 25; 144 L.T. 441; 47 T.L.R. 147; 30 Com. Cas. 159; 18 Asp. M.L.C. 184, H.L. 25

Fink-Frucht G.m.b.H. *v.* Hauptzollamt München-Landsbergerstrasse, 27/67, [1968] C.M.L.R. 228; 14 Recueil 341–2 .. .. 19, 21

Fraz Grad *v.* Finanzamt Traunstein, 2/70, [1971] C.M.L.R. 1 20

Gouvernement de la République Italienne *v.* Haute Autorité, 20/59 (1960), 6 Recueil 687 21

Gouvernement du Royaume des Pays-Bas *v.* Haute Autorité (1960), 6 Recueil 756 .. 21

Haselhorst *v.* Finanzamt Düsseldorf-Altstadt, 23/70, [1971] C.M.L.R. 1 20

Kelner *v.* Baxter (1866), L.R. 2 C.P. 174; 36 L.J.C.P. 94; 15 L.T. 213; 15 W.R. 278; 12 Jur. N.S. 1016 .. .. 37.3

Lütticke *v.* Hauptzollamt de Sarrelouis, 57/65, [1971] C.M.L.R. 674; 12 Recueil 294 18, 21

Mölkerei-Zentrale Westfalen/Lippe G.m.b.H. *v.* Hauptzollamt Paderborn 28/67, [1968] C.M.L.R. 187; 6 C.M.L. Rev. 132; 14 Recueil 212 .. .. 18, 21

Newborne *v.* Sensolid (Great Britain), Ltd., [1954] 1 Q.B. 45; [1953] 1 All E.R. 708; [1953] 2 W.L.R. 596; 97 Sol. Jo. 209, C.A. 36.3

Post Office *v.* Estuary Radio, Ltd., [1968] 2 Q.B. 740; [1967] 3 All E.R. at p. 679; [1967] 1 W.L.R. 1396; 111 Sol. Jo. 636; [1967] 2 Lloyd's Rep. 299, C.A. .. 24

S.A.C.E. *v.* Italian Ministry of Finance, 33/70, [1971] C.M.L.R. 123.. 19, 20

Salgoil *v.* Ministère du Commerce Extérieur de la République Italienne, 13/68, [1969] C.M.L.R. 181; 14 Recueil 673 .. .. 19, 21

S.A.S. Eunomia di Porro E.C. *v.* Ministro della Pubblico Istruzione, 18/71 .. 19

Salomon *v.* Customs and Excise Commissioners, [1967] 2 Q.B. 116; [1966] 3 All E.R. 871; [1966] 3 W.L.R. 1223; 110 Sol. Jo. 833, C.A. 24, 25

Transports Lesage et Cie. *v.* Hauptzollamt Freiburg, 20/70, [1971] C.M.L.R. 1 .. 20

Van Gend en Loos *v.* Nederlandsee Belastingadministratie, 26/62, [1963] C.M.L.R. 105; 9 Recueil 22 .. .. 19, 21

Wakefield and District Light Railways Co. *v.* Wakefield Corporation, [1906] 2 K.B. 140; affirmed, [1907] 2 K.B. 256; 76 L.J.K.B. 634; 71 J.P. 254; 96 L.T. 622; 23 T.L.R. 404; 5 L.G.R. 595, C.A.; *sub nom.* Wakefield Corporation *v.* Wakefield and District Light Rail. Co., [1908] A.C. 293; 77 L.J.K.B. 692; 99 L.T. 1; 72 J.P. 315; 24 T.L.R. 603; 52 Sol. Jo. 497; 6 L.G.R. 647; 2 Konst. Rat. App. 433, H.L. 29.2

DIVISION I

INTRODUCTION

DIVISION I

INTRODUCTION

[**1**] The European Communities Act 1972, in making "provision in connection with the enlargement of the European Communities to include the United Kingdom, together with (for certain purposes) the Channel Islands, the Isle of Man and Gibraltar", has a twofold task. First, it must make general provision enabling the law of the Communities to be implemented as required by the Community Treaties including the Treaty and Act of Accession. Secondly it must make substantive amendments in certain areas of United Kingdom law to render it compatible with, or to enable it directly to implement, Community law as from the 1st January 1973—or later, as required by the Transitional Measures of the Act of Accession.

[**2**] Part I of the Act makes the necessary general provision. Part II is concerned with the second part of the task, the substantive amendment of United Kingdom law in eight distinct areas: Customs duties, the common agricultural policy, sugar, cinematograph films, companies, restrictive trade practices, Community offences and the furnishing of information to the Communities. Although the number of areas of United Kingdom law that may be or become subject to the impact of Community law is likely to be limited, those eight in regard to which Part II makes provision do not exhaust the list. For those that may remain, provision will normally be able to be made under Part I, though it may be noted that legislation as to Value Added Tax, for example, must (for reasons explained in the comments to s. 2, [**30.3**], *post*) be by way of quite separate enactment from the present Act.

[**3**] That the European Communities Act contains much that is novel in United Kingdom legislation need hardly be said. That novelty is in general a reflection, and frequently, in particular sections of the Act, a result of the novelty of the legal techniques and concepts that found expression in the three treaties establishing respectively the European Coal and Steel Community (in 1952) and the European Economic Community as well as the European Atomic Energy Community ("Euratom") in 1958.

THE NOVELTY OF THE ORIGINAL THREE COMMUNITY TREATIES

[**4**] These three treaties were unlike any international treaties that had ever previously been made—not merely as to their objects, which were novel enough,

but even more in the legal mechanisms which they established for achieving those objects.

[**5**] Hitherto, any treaty had always been concerned essentially with what a signatory State must or must not do in its external relations, that is to say, in its dealings with other signatory States and in its dealings with non-signatory States. It was in the external relations of States, as international persons in the sense of international law, that treaties produced their primary and direct legal effects. For if adaptation of the domestic or internal law of a signatory State were necessary to enable that State to fulfil its treaty obligations, such consequential adaptation was effected by suitable internal legislation and not directly by the treaty itself, which remained, so to speak, at one remove. In the United Kingdom, treaty making was and remains the prerogative of the Monarch and His or Her Ministers, whereas any adaptation of domestic law within the United Kingdom, made necessary for the State to comply with a treaty so made, requires Parliamentary approval of the objects of the treaty and the enactment by Parliament of the internal legislation consequentially necessary. Thus, for example, when the United Kingdom, in 1944 became a party to the Agreement establishing the International Monetary Fund, consequential internal legislation also became necessary.

[**6**] The foregoing considerations highlight one part of the novelty of the three European Community Treaties. Like other treaties before them, they produce their effects in the external relations of each ratifying State: they lay down what such a State must and must not do in its relations with the other ratifying States and what it may and may not do in its relations with non-signatory States. But the three Treaties go further. They lay down, in general terms and for certain defined and limited purposes, how a ratifying State must order its internal affairs. They go even further than that, and herein lies the greatest novelty. They themselves take direct effect for certain purposes within each ratifying State, thereby bringing about, by their own legal force, a re-ordering of certain aspects of that State's internal law without there being need for, or indeed the possibility of, consequential internal legislation to effect that re-ordering. In other words, the impact which the Treaties make upon a ratifying State is threefold:

(1) They affect its external relations, as a matter of international law;
(2) they impose obligations upon that State to make adjustments in its internal legal order; and
(3) they enter into force, as to many of their provisions, automatically, as a new component *within* that internal legal order—without any legislative intervention by that State to bring about that result.

[**7**] The European Communities Act reflects that threefold impact on the United Kingdom as a result of its accession to the European Communities. But the Act is not, and cannot be, more than indirectly, concerned with the primary impact which relates to matters of international law. Its concern with the second point is direct; it is itself the enactment whereby the adjustments are either made or made possible. As to the third point, the Act does not, and does

not need to, provide for the bringing about of the entry into force, within the legal order of the United Kingdom, of those provisions of Community law which are directly applicable within that order—but it does provide, in recognition of their entry into force within the United Kingdom legal order, how effect is to be given to them. A clear understanding of the Act requires that the distinction between the second and third points—between the indirect and the direct effects of Community law in internal law be constantly borne in mind.

[**8**] These effects, like the distinction between them, derive from the substance, including the objects, of what the Act defines as "the Treaties" or "Community Treaties". They derive ultimately from the three original Treaties listed in the opening paragraph of this Introduction (and as 1, 2, and 3 in Schedule I, Part 1, of the Act). More immediately, they derive, in the words of section 1 (2) of the Act, from "the treaty relating to the accession of the United Kingdom to the European Economic Community and to the European Atomic Energy Community . . . and the Decision . . . of the Council of the European Communities relating to the accession of the United Kingdom to the European Coal and Steel Community and any other treaty entered into by any of the Communities, with or without any of the member States, or entered into, as a treaty ancillary to any of the Treaties, by the United Kingdom . . .". It is "taken with" all of these that the "pre-accession treaties, that is to say, those described in Part I of Schedule 1 to the Act" acquire, and by virtue of section 1 (2) are to have in the Act, the meaning "the Treaties" or "the Community Treaties".

DIRECT AND INDIRECT EFFECTS OF THE TREATIES WITHIN A MEMBER STATE OF THE COMMUNITIES

[**9**] The distinction—to the importance of which reference has just been made—between the direct effects and the indirect effects of "the Treaties" is revealed in the very first provisions of substance in the Act, that is, in section 2. Sub-section (1), dealing with direct effects, is concerned with "All such rights, powers, liabilities, obligations and restrictions from time to time created or arising by or under the Treaties, and all such remedies and procedures from time to time provided for by or under the Treaties, as in accordance with the Treaties are without further enactment to be given legal effect or used in the United Kingdom . . .". Sub-section (2), dealing with indirect effects, is concerned with "implementing any Community obligation of the United Kingdom, or enabling any such obligation to be implemented, or of enabling any rights enjoyed or to be enjoyed by the United Kingdom under or by virtue of the Treaties to be exercised" as well as with related or other matters. It may be noted in passing that one aspect of the distinction is manifest in the difference that sub-section (1) deals with legal effects *in* the United Kingdom, whereas sub-section (2) is concerned with obligations *of* the United Kingdom and rights enjoyable *by* the United Kingdom.

[**10**] Though sub-sections (1) and (2) thus reflect a very marked distinction, they are, in one feature, alike. Sub-section (1) is concerned with "all such

rights, powers, liabilities, obligations and restrictions *from time to time* created or arising . . ." and sub-section (2) is concerned with what may be done "*at any time*" after the passing of the Act, specifying in its last paragraph that "In this subsection 'designated Minister or department' means such Minister of the Crown or government department as may *from time to time* be designated by Order in Council". As is implied or expressed throughout the Act as a whole, the legal effects within the United Kingdom and upon the United Kingdom, for which the two sub-sections respectively make such explicit provisions, are not once and for all effects. For they derive from an ultimate source which is not like an extinct volcano, but like one which must be expected to erupt at any time or from time to time. What, then, is that source?

EACH COMMUNITY AN AUTONOMOUS LEGAL ORDER

[11] The source, obviously, is the three European Communities to which the United Kingdom has acceded by the Treaty signed in Brussels on 22nd January 1972. To be more adequate, the answer requires an assessment of the *legal* meaning of "Community"—not an analysis of the *economic* phenomena which the establishment of the Communities has brought or is bringing about, such as the common market, the customs union, the agricultural policy, the commercial policy, and so on.

[12] Upon ratification and entry into force of the respective original Treaty, of 1951 or 1957, each Community was established, immediately, complete with all its legal attributes, as a nexus of legal rights and obligations, provided for in the treaty, exercisable or owed by (1) all natural and legal persons within the treaty's ambit, or (2) by the member States of the Community (additionally to their obligations and rights relative to the Community *per se*), or (3) by the Institutions of the Community, within a criss-cross multilateral legal order bringing, or capable of bringing, persons in any of (1) to (3) into direct legal relationship, as a matter of Community law, with persons in any of (1) to (3), as provided in the treaty, or as determined by the secondary legislation of the Community itself.

[13] That each Community was empowered, by the treaty, to originate its own secondary legislation is one measure of the legal autonomy conferred upon it, as an act of sovereign volition, by the founding States (and explains why, in the metaphor used above, the volcano must be expected to erupt at any time, and from time to time). Its autonomy is further exemplified and re-inforced by the attributes of the Institutions of the Community, established by the same treaty—notably the complete independence of the Commission from the member States of the Community, and, above all, the complete independence of the Court of Justice of the Community, not only from the member States, but also from each of the other Institutions (as well as, of course, from the natural and legal persons otherwise within the Community nexus). So, each Community constitutes an autonomous legal order, having as its substantive law the law of the treaty by which it is established, as further developed by autonomously originated secondary legislation in accordance with that treaty, and having autonomous Institutions, on the one hand to originate that secondary legislation and, on the other hand, to ensure that the law is observed in the interpretation and application of the treaty and of the secondary legislation. That each Community is an autonomous legal order has been repeatedly stressed by the European Court (the Court of Justice of the European Communities, to give it its formal name) in such judgments as No. 26/62 *Van Gend en Loos* v. *Netherlands Fiscal Administration*; 6/64 *Costa* v. *E.N.E.L.*; 28/67 *Molkerei-Zentrale Westfalen-Lippe G.M.B.H.* v. *Hauptzollamt Paderborn.*

[**14**] The enlargement of the Communities to number nine member States, by the accession of the United Kingdom, Denmark and Eire, has in no way affected the fundamental principle that they each constitute an autonomous legal order. The nexus of legal rights and obligations, in the sense referred to two paragraphs earlier, is extended to embrace not only the new member States but the natural and legal persons whom these States bring with them into the Communities. The substantive law, that of the treaties and of the Community secondary legislation, applies, subject to transitional provisions in the Treaty of Accession, both to and within the new member States. Of the correctness of the application of Community law, within the new, as within the original, member States, the European Court is the final arbiter.

[**15**] Since the extension of the nexus to natural and legal persons within the United Kingdom brings them into direct legal relationship, actual or potential, with the Institutions of the Communities; since substantive Community law does, or may, impose upon the United Kingdom obligations in respect of persons subject to its jurisdiction; since substantive Community law does confer rights upon such persons, over against United Kingdom authorities, that if need be they are entitled to apply to United Kingdom courts to enforce—for these and similar reasons it is clear that the impact of Community law must be made *within* the United Kingdom (and the countries joining the Communities together with it) and not merely *upon* them. It also clearly follows that in making that direct impact within the United Kingdom legal order, Community law must prevail over it in case of conflict—somewhat in the manner that equity prevails over the common law—if the aims of the Treaties are to be fulfilled and the obligations of the United Kingdom thereunder are to be met.

DIRECTLY APPLICABLE COMMUNITY LAW

[**16**] The expression "directly applicable Community provision" occurs at frequent intervals throughout the Act, eleven times in all.[1] Yet it does not figure amongst the Definitions set out in Schedule 1, nor is it defined in any section of the Act. This is not a lacuna in the Act, for there is to be noted in this absence, as in all other particulars, the scrupulous regard of the Act for the dichotomy between the two independent legal orders—that of the Communities on the one hand, and, on the other hand, that of the United Kingdom, in which

[1] Ss. 5 (1) (Customs Duties); 6 (4) (Common Agricultural Policy); 7 (1) and (2) Sugar; 10 (1) and (2) (Restrictive Practices); Schedule 1, Part II (in the Definition of "Community customs duty"); in Schedule 4, para. 3 (2) (*a*) in amending Food and Drugs Act 1955, s. 123; 9 (1) in amending Road Traffic Act 1972, s. 4 (4); 10 in amending Road Traffic (International Passenger Services) Act 1960, s. 161 (1).

alone the Act can take effect. The absence of a definition of "directly applicable Community provision" not only bears testimony to that dichotomy; it implicitly indicates that the expression describes a concept of *Community* law, which alone can define its meaning. And where the Act uses the expression, it does so merely descriptively, to refer to a concept appertaining to a legal order distinct from that to which it belongs itself.

[**17**] In Community law, the essence of the concept of provisions of that legal order being directly applicable in the legal order of each of the member States of the Communities is clear enough—and has been, if not from the earliest days (though by Article 15 of the Coal and Steel Community Treaty of 1952 general decisions of the High Authority "take effect by the mere fact of publication") certainly from 1958, when Article 189 of the Economic Community Treaty, and Article 161 of the Euratom Treaty, laid down more maturely: "A regulation shall have general application. It shall be binding in its entirety and directly applicable in all member States". But if the essence of the concept was always clear in regard to Community Regulations—or to General Decisions of the High Authority which, in kind, are no different—it is as a result of the decisions rendered by the European Court that the concept of "direct applicability" has been progressively further clarified (though not made the subject of an exhaustive definition) and that some provisions other than Regulations and General Decisions are now recognised in Community law as being directly applicable in the legal order of member States (for example, certain Articles of the Treaties themselves, and even certain Directives or, less assuredly, certain (individual) decisions).

[**18**] It is thus now established, as a matter of Community law, that a directly applicable provision of that law is not merely a provision of an independent legal order which requires to be *followed* in the legal orders of Community member States. It is a provision which in fact *penetrates into* and *takes effect within* those legal orders, distinct though they are from the Community legal order in which it originates. It is at this point that the possibility arises of conflict between the directly applicable Community provision and provisions of the legal order of a member State into which it penetrates. Part of the purpose of the European Communities Act is to ensure to the maximum extent the avoidance of such conflict. It is, however, obvious that if the objects of the Community Treaties are to be fulfilled, any conflicts that do arise between the legal order of the United Kingdom and a provision of Community law directly applicable in that order must always be resolved by permitting the Community provision to prevail. The European Court has on several occasions delivered an unequivocal ruling in this sense[2] (thereby constituting one of "the principles laid down by" it, within the meaning of s. 3 (1) of the Act —to be followed "in all legal proceedings"). In so doing it has also demonstrated what has been described[3] as the "close, functional, relation to the supremacy of Community law" of the direct applicability of some of its provisions. The function of a

[2] Strikingly, in case no. 6/64, *Costa* v. *E.N.E.L.*, [1964] C.M.L.R. 425; X Recueil, 1143 at p. 1159.

[3] Bebr. I.C.L.Q., Vol. 19, 1970, p. 262.

directly applicable Community provision is, in the words of the Court, to have, in the legal order of member States, "direct effects, and give rise to rights of individuals, which the national courts must respect".[4]

[**19**] The characteristics of a Community provision that are requisite if it is to be directly applicable in member States have already been, and will no doubt continue to be, clarified by decisions of the European Court, though it has never formulated a complete definition. The first requisite characteristic is that the provision must be, in the Court's customary formula "complete and legally perfect".[5] But whether or not a provision in a Community *Treaty* is perfect in this sense does not depend on its wording alone, but on its "spirit, structure, and wording".[6] The fact that a Treaty provision is explicitly addressed to member States does not prevent its being directly applicable,[7] nor is its direct applicability excluded by its being formally so addressed.[8] But it must be clear and precise, subject to no conditions, and require no further measures either on the part of the Community institutions or on the part of the member States—or at at least, if required to be taken by member States, the latter have no discretion under Community law that could permit them to avoid taking those measures. Some of the E.E.C. Treaty provisions which prohibit member States from taking certain courses of action (e.g. Articles 12; 31 and 32, para. 1; 37 (2); 53 and 95 (1); see the cases in footnote 7) have been held by the Court to be directly applicable; other provisions imposing prohibitions on member States (e.g. Articles 32 (2) and 33—see case no. 13/68 in footnote 7), however, have been held by the Court to be insufficiently clear to be directly applicable.

[**20**] It would seem to be obvious that to be directly applicable a Community provision must be unconditional and that is perhaps why Community provisions imposing prohibitions on member States have on the whole, as the above examples show, fairly readily been held by the European Court to be directly applicable. But these cases concerned provisions in the Treaties themselves. There is as yet little clarification to be found in the case law of the Court

---

[4] In No. 26/62, *Van Gend en Loos* v. *Netherlands Fiscal Administration,* [1963] C.M.L.R. 106; IX Recueil 3 at p. 25 (interpreting Art. 12 of E.C. Treaty). See also Nos. 57/65, *Lütticke* v. *Hauptzollamt de Sarrelouis,* [1971] C.M.L.R. 674, (1966) XII Recueil 294 at p. 304; 28/67, *Molkerei-Zentrale* v. *Hauptzollamt Paderborn,* [1968] C.M.L.R. 187, XIV Recueil 212 at p. 232.

[5] See decision in No. 57/65 *Lütticke,* [1971] C.M.L.R. 674; (1966) XII Recueil at p. 302.

[6] In No. 26/62 *Van Gend en Loos* v. *Netherlands Fiscal Administration,* [1963] C.M.L.R. 106, IX Recueil at pp. 22 and 25, and in No. 28/67 *Molkerei-Zentrale Westfalen* v. *Hauptzollamt Paderborn,* [1968] C.M.L.R. 187; XIV Recueil at p. 226.

[7] Thus the European Court in considering E.E.C. Treaty, Articles 9 and 13 (2) in No. 33/70 *S.A.C.E.* v. *Italian Ministry of Finances* [1971] C.M.L.R. 123; Article 12 in No. 26/62 *Van Gend en Loos* (1963), IX Recueil 3 at p. 24; Article 16 in No. 18/71 *S.A.S. Eunomia di Porro E.C.* v. *Ministro della Pubblica Istruzione*; Articles 53 and 37 (2) in No. 6/64 *Costa* v. *E.N.E.L.,* [1964] C.M.L.R. 425; X Recueil at pp. 1162 and 1164 respectively; Article 95, paras. 1 and 3 in No. 57/65 *Lütticke,* [1971] C.M.L.R. 674, (1966) XII Recueil at pp. 302–3; Article 95, para. 2 in No. 27/67 *Fink-Frucht* v. *Hauptzollamt München-Landsbergerstrasse,* [1968] C.M.L.R. 228, XIV Recueil at pp. 341–2; Articles 31 and 32, para. 1 in No. 13/68 *Salgoil* v. *Ministère du Commerce Extérieur de la République Italienne,* [1969] C.M.L.R. 181, (1968) XIV Recueil at p. 673.

[8] No. 26/62 *Van Gend en Loos* (1963), IX Recueil at p. 24; No. 57/65 *Lütticke,* [1971] C.M.L.R. 674, (1966) XII Recueil at p. 302; No. 28/67 *Molkerei-Zentrale Westfalen* (1968), C.M.L.R. 187, XIV Recueil at p. 226.

regarding the direct applicability of Community Decisions and Directives,[9] though from such pointers as there are it appears that to a limited extent such of these as impose a prohibition on a member State, or a clear (and simple?) obligation, would be likely to be held to be directly applicable.

[**21**] Another aspect of direct applicability which it may be hoped the European Court will soon have further opportunity to clarify, concerns Community Regulations, and provisions in the Treaties themselves. As the Court has held in a line of cases over a period of some 8–9 years,[10] a Treaty provision may be directly applicable in the legal order of member States provided no further measure by either the member States or the Community has first to be taken. (One of the reasons why Community provisions imposing a prohibition on member States have been fairly readily held by the European Court to be directly applicable—as shown above—is precisely that a prohibition, by its nature, requires no further action for it to be complete). In conformity with that view, the Court[11] rejected the contention that a Treaty Article was directly applicable, because in fact further measures were required, and later more specifically ruled that no such measures must be required either on the part of the member State[12] or that of the Community.[10] What measures are to be regarded as within the concept of "further measures" remains to be more completely clarified; but from the cases (cases 28/67 and 13/68)[10] it is already clear that where a Community provision leaves a discretion, to either member State or Community institutions, to take the measures necessary for its implementation, the provision cannot in principle be directly applicable.

[**22**] With regard to Community Regulations, direct applicability is a more complex matter than the Treaty definition of Regulation, already referred to, would at first sight indicate. For, although by that definition (E.E.C. Treaty, Article 189 and Euratom Treaty, Article 161) a Regulation "shall be binding in its entirety and directly applicable in all member States; such applicability may encounter two kinds of difficulty in practice. In the first place, it is clearly not the form of a Regulation, but its substance, which makes it directly applicable; it must therefore not only be duly published or issued in the form and manner required by Community law, but must be what the European Court has described[13] as a "true" or "real" Regulation. Secondly, the Com-

---

[9] The reader should, however, refer to the following cases: No. 9/70 (*Franz Grad* v. *Finanzamt Traunstein*, [1971] C.M.L.R. 1, No. 20/70 *Transports Lesage et Cie.* v. *Hauptzollamt Freiburg*, [1971] C.M.L.R. 1, No. 23/70 *Erich Haselhorst* v. *Finanzamt Düsseldorf*, [1971] C.M.L.R. 1 and as to a Directive, No. 33/70 *S.A.C.E.* v. *Ministero delle Finanze*, [1971] C.M.L.R. 123.

[10] Judgments in cases: No. 26/62 *Van Gend en Loos*, [1963] C.M.L.R. 105, IX Recueil 3 at p. 24; No. 6/64 *Costa* v. *E.N.E.L.*, [1964] C.M.L.R. 425, X Recueil at pp. 1162, 1164; No. 57/65 *Lütticke*, [1971] C.M.L.R. 674; (1966) XII Recueil at p. 302; No. 28/67 *Molkerei-Zentrale Westfalen*, [1968] C.M.L.R. 187, XIV Recueil at p. 226; No. 27/67 *Fink-Frucht*, [1968] C.M.L.R. 228, XIV Recueil at pp. 341–2; No. 13/68 *Salgoil*, [1969] C.M.L.R. 181, (1968) XIV Recueil at p. 673.

[11] E.C.S.C. Treaty, Art. 70 (3), in Nos: 20/59 *Gouvernement de la République Italienne* v. *Haute Autorité* (1960), VI Recueil at p. 687, and 25/59 *Gouvernement du Royaume des Pays-Bas* v. *Haute Autorité* (1960), VI Recueil at p. 756.

[12] Judgment in No. 26/62 *Van Gend en Loos*, IX Recueil at p. 24.

[13] In No. 16–17/62 *Confédération Nationale des producteurs de fruits et Légumes* v. *Conseil de la C.E.E.*, [1963] C.M.L.R. 160; (1962) VIII Recueil at p. 20 ("véritables règlements").

munity institutions have long recognised the fact that Regulations may frequently need further measures to be taken by member States in order that they may take effect (and Regulations are consequently often made with a closing formula—virtually standard form—requiring member States to take them). This aspect does not lend itself to exhaustive treatment in an Introduction, but the notes[14] in the main text should, it is hoped, enable the user of this book readily to identify any particular problem relating thereto arising under the present Act and to pusue it as necessary in fuller works on Community law.

CONSTRUCTION AND INTERPRETATION

[**23**] The operation of the Act in practice may perhaps be expected to highlight the role of the rules of United Kingdom law concerning the construction of statutes, particularly in respect of the extent of the recourse which is thereunder permissible to the Treaties which the Act is expressly concerned to implement, and to the secondary legislation of the Communities for the implementation of which it makes provision. Probably the question of the extent of the permissible recourse to Community law for purposes of construction may be posed most acutely by the operation in United Kingdom law of directly applicable Community law (as has been implicit in the brief discussion of Community Regulations in the preceding paragraph), but the possibility certainly cannot be ruled out of the same question arising in respect of the implementation by United Kingdom legal measures of Community law which is not directly applicable but requires such complementary measures, nor, indeed, the possibility of its arising in respect of the Act itself.

[**24**] The question is, of course, one for the courts themselves. They have not as yet had it before them in relation to treaty law of the directly applicable nature of some Community law, which penetrates *into* United Kingdom law. But latterly they have needed to resolve it in regard to a treaty of the more traditional kind. "In *Salomon* v. *Customs and Excise Commissioners* [1967] 2 Q.B. 116, the Court of Appeal has recently made clear that where there is cogent extrinsic evidence of a connection between an international treaty and an Act under interpretation, a court may look at the Convention in elucidating the Act, although the Act nowhere makes mention of the treaty. And in *Post Office* v. *Estuary Radio Ltd.*, [1968] 2 Q.B. 740, the Court of Appeal held that where the meaning of the domestic legislation (in the case, the Territorial Waters Order in Council, 1964) is not clear, it should be construed in the light of the treaty to which it is giving effect, having regard to the presumption that the national authority (here the Crown) intends to carry out its international obligations.[15]

[**25**] It is apparent at once that the connection between the Community Treaties and the European Communities Act is not, as in the *Salomon* case

---

[14] See, for example, under s. 2 (1) WITHOUT FURTHER ENACTMENT, and in Sched. 1, Part II, COMMUNITY OBLIGATION.

[15] From the Law Commission report on the Interpretation of Statutes, 9 June 1969, pp. 8, 9.

above, a matter of "cogent extrinsic evidence" but of cogent intrinsic evidence—the Long Title[16] of the Act, the Heading of Part II, and Section 1, amply provide it. Nevertheless, as has been pointed out earlier in this Introduction, the present Act has scrupulous regard for the dichotomy between Community law on the one hand and United Kingdom law on the other hand and it is suggested that consequently the Act should, in general, for purposes of construction of its own provisions or of those made under it, be made to stand on its own feet alone. Furthermore, there would remain at least to consider, in relation to the *Salomon* case above, *Ellerman Lines* v. *Murray*, [1931] A.C. 126 and also *Attorney-General* v. *Prince Ernest Augustus of Hanover*, [1957] A.C. 436 at p. 473. There is also the appropriate comment[17] that "even in a case with an international content such as *Salomon* it is only where the words of the provision to be interpreted are 'reasonably capable of more than one meaning' (*per* DIPLOCK L. J.) that the treaty becomes relevant. This does not seem to deal with the situation where the words of a provision, in the context of the national instrument alone, appear reasonably to have only one meaning, although in the wider context of a treaty they might offer a choice of meanings."

[**26**] As was suggested three paragraphs earlier, probably the most acute form in which this question of construction may present itself is in respect of Community provisions that are directly applicable in United Kingdom law. In fact, it will be seen that should the question present itself in this connection, the question itself may be modified by that connection. It may become a question of deciding whether, or when, a provision of Community law, penetrating thus into United Kingdom law, becomes, as a result, subject itself to construction as if it were in fact United Kingdom law (and had been since its origin). This would appear to be so when a United Kingdom instrument actually incorporates the Community provision, whether textually or by reference. Where the Community provision is not so incorporated but the United Kingdom instrument, by "cogent extrinsic evidence", is shown to be connected with it, then the principle in the *Salomon* case above becomes at least relevant—unless it is held that, the Community provision being directly applicable, recourse to that principle is unnecessary. Where the Community provision is by Treaty Definition (e.g. a Directive, E.E.C. Treaty, Art. 189) *not* directly applicable, very much the same question may nevertheless arise where it is contended that a prohibition, imposed on the United Kingdom, is not honoured in United Kingdom measures complementary to that Community provision.

[**27**] In regard to this matter, developments in the case law, both of the United Kingdom and of that of the European Court, must be awaited—and are perhaps to be expected.

---

[16] "In interpreting a particular provision of a statute there is no doubt that a court may consider the context provided by other enacting provisions of the same statute, the long title, and the preamble. The interpretative status of the short title, although enacted by Parliament, is uncertain"—the Law Commission report, *idem* p. 26 (see *Re Boaler*, [1915] 1 K.B. 21, (C.A). Contrast conflicting dicta of BUCKLEY L.J. at p. 27 and SCRUTTON L.J. at pp. 40–41).

[17] Of the Law Commission, *idem* p. 10.

DIVISION II

EUROPEAN COMMUNITIES ACT 1972

EUROPEAN COMMUNITIES ACT 1972

(1971 c. 68)

ARRANGEMENT OF SECTIONS

PART I

GENERAL PROVISIONS

Section		Para.
1.	Short title and interpretation	[29]
2.	General implementation of Treaties	[30]
3.	Decisions on, and proof of, Treaties and Community instruments etc.	[31]

PART II

AMENDMENT OF LAW

4.	General provision for repeal and amendment	[32]
5.	Customs duties	[33]
6.	The common agricultural policy	[34]
7.	Sugar	[35]
8.	Cinematograph films	[36]
9.	Companies	[37]
10.	Restrictive trade practices	[38]
11.	Community offences	[39]
12.	Furnishing of information to Communities	[40]

SCHEDULES:

Schedule 1—Definitions relating to Communities	[41–56]
Schedule 2—Provisions as to subordinate legislation	[57–59]
Schedule 3—Repeals	[60]
Schedule 4—Enactments amended	[61–70]

An Act to make provision in connection with the enlargement of the European Communities to include the United Kingdom, together with (for certain purposes) the Channel Islands, the Isle of Man and Gibraltar

[17th October 1972] **[28]**

THE LONG TITLE

The formulation of the Long Title supplies the general nexus between, on the one hand, the legal order of the United Kingdom, and, on the other hand, the legal order of the Communities—the dichotomy between which legal orders the substance of the Act scrupulously respects. For example, the Long Title together with the Heading of Part II of the Act ("Amendment of Law") supplies such a nexus where, on the face of some of the provisions in that Part (e.g. s. 9), there is none apparent.

THE CHANNEL ISLANDS AND THE ISLE OF MAN

As to the application to these of the E.C.S.C. Treaty, see Art. 25 of the Act annexed to the Accession Treaty of 22nd January 1972; as to the application to them of the E.E.C. Treaty, see *idem* Art. 26; as to the application to them of the Euratom Treaty, see *idem* Art. 27. These three articles provide that the respective Treaty shall apply to them (the islands) "only to the extent necessary to ensure the implementation of the arrangements for those islands set out in "the Decision concerning accession to the E.C.S.C. or the Treaty concerning E.E.C. and Euratom. The arrangements are set out in Protocol No. 3 of the Act of Accession (pp. 82–84, Cmnd. 4862–1). The broad effect of the arrangements is to place the islands in the same position as the United Kingdom in respect of the Community customs regime, and to make the Community agricultural provisions apply to them in principle and dependent in practice on subsequent Community measures. [**28.1**]

GIBRALTAR

The position of Gibraltar with respect to the Communities is in general the same as that of the United Kingdom, but subject to the following exceptions:

1. Gibraltar is not included in the customs territory of the enlarged E.E.C. Community (because of its status as a free port). It does not figure in the list of countries comprising that customs territory in Art. 1 of E.E.C. Council Regulation 1496/68 of 27 September 1968, as adapted by virtue of Art. 29 of the Act of Accession and as set out in Annex I to that Act (at pp. 5–6 of Cmnd. 4862–11).
2. By Art. 28 of the Act annexed to the Treaty of Accession, Gibraltar is excluded from the application of certain acts of the institutions of the Community. Broadly speaking the effect is that Gibraltar is excluded from the Agricultural Regulations, from acts relating to processed foods, and from harmonisation provisions relating to legislation in respect of turnover taxes (V.A.T.).
3. In respect of the E.E.C. Community's commercial policy, "the problem created by the deletion of the reference to Gibraltar in Annex II is to be solved in such a way as to ensure that Gibraltar is in the same position with regard to the Community's import liberalisation system as it was before accession" (Cmnd. 4862–11, p. 141). These are the "guidelines" in conformity with which Annex II to the Act of Accession provides for the adaptation in respect of Gibraltar of E.E.C. Council Regulation 1025/70 of 25 May 1970, as modified by E.E.C. Council Regulations 1984/70 of 29 September 1970, 724/71 of 31 March 1971, 1080/71 of 25 May 1971, 1429/71 of 2 July 1971 and 2384/71 of 8 November 1971. The matter is in regard to third countries which have accepted certain Community liberalisation measures.

(Unlike Art. 29 of the Act of Accession, which specifies the adaptations to be made to certain acts of Community institutions, listed in Annex 1 to that Act (in the manner exemplified in 1 above), Art. 30 of the same provides for adaptations to other acts, of Community institutions, listed in Annex II, to be made "in conformity with the guidelines set out in that Annex . . .")

In consequence of the Channel Islands, the Isle of Man and Gibraltar being, in general, in the same position as the United Kingdom in relation to the Communities, s. 2 (6) provides that any law passed by the legislature of any of those Islands, or any colonial law made or passed for Gibraltar "if expressed to be passed or made in the implementation of the Treaties", as defined in s. 1 (2), "shall not be void or inoperative by reason of any inconsistency with or repugnancy to an Act of Parliament, passed or to be passed, that extends to the Island or Gibraltar . . ." S. 4 (4) provides for the extension, or the possibility of extension, to the Channel Islands or the Isle of Man, of the repeal or amendment of an existing enactment (as provided by Sched. 3 or 4 to the Act) that itself so extends or is capable of being extended. [**28.2**]

Part I

General Provisions

GENERAL NOTE

Treaties constitute by far the most important source of the law of the European Communities. The first purpose of Part I is to specify (by s.1, together with Sched. 1, Part 1) those Treaties which are the source of Community law, and the implementation of which, by and in the United Kingdom, must be provided for by the Act.

(S. 2 makes provision (in sub-s. (1)) for the enforceability in the United Kingdom of rights and obligations (and powers, liabilities and restrictions) arising under the Treaties or created by them, and (in sub-s. (2)) for the implementation of Community obligations of the United Kingdom and for the enjoyment by it of rights created by or arising under the Treaties. Sub-s. (3) makes provision for payments, required by any Community obligation, to the Communities or to member States, and payments in respect of the European Investment Bank, as well as for receipts and other expenditure under the Treaties. Sub-s. (4) makes provision as to the construction of Part II of the Act, and for Sched. 2 to have effect in connection with the powers to make Orders in Council or regulations that are conferred by any of ss. 2–12 of the Act. Sub-s. (5) provides for legislation in Northern Ireland in implementation of Community obligations, and sub-s. (6) makes corresponding provision in respect of the Channel Islands, the Isle of Man and Gibraltar.

S. 3 makes provision as to decisions on and proof of Community instruments in all legal proceedings. It requires judicial notice to be taken (*inter alia*) of decisions, or expressions of opinions, by the European Court. It requires the principles laid down by that Court, and any relevant decision it has rendered, to be followed in determining as a matter of law "any question as to the meaning or effect of any of the Treaties, or as to the validity, meaning or effect of any Community instrument".

Part I is not an entrenched provision.

1. Short title and interpretation

(1) This Act may be cited as the European Communities Act 1972.

(2) In this Act and, except in so far as the context otherwise requires, in any other Act (including any Act of the Parliament of Northern Ireland)—

"the Communities" means the European Economic Community, the European Coal and Steel Community and the European Atomic Energy Community;

"the Treaties" or "the Community Treaties" means, subject to subsection (3) below, the pre-accession treaties, that is to say, those described in Part I of Schedule 1 to this Act, taken with—

(*a*) the treaty relating to the accession of the United Kingdom to the European Economic Community and to the European Atomic Energy Community, signed at Brussels on the 22nd January 1972; and

(*b*) the decision, of the same date, of the Council of the European Communities relating to the accession of the United Kingdom to the European Coal and Steel Community;

and any other treaty entered into by any of the Communities, with or without any of the member States, or entered into, as a treaty ancillary to any of the Treaties, by the United Kingdom;

and any expression defined in Schedule 1 to this Act has the meaning there given to it.

(3) If Her Majesty by Order in Council declares that a treaty specified in the Order is to be regarded as one of the Community Treaties as herein defined, the Order shall be conclusive that it is to be so regarded; but a treaty entered into by the United Kingdom after the 22nd January 1972, other than a pre-accession treaty to which the United Kingdom accedes on terms settled on or before that date, shall not be so regarded unless it is so specified, nor be so specified unless a draft of the Order in Council has been approved by resolution of each House of Parliament.

(4) For purposes of subsections (2) and (3) above, "treaty" includes any international agreement, and any protocol or annex to a treaty or international agreement. **[29]**

SUB-S. (2): GENERAL NOTE

Treaties constitute the primary source of the law of the European Communities. The purpose of the subsection is to make ascertainable the Treaties that must be implemented by or in the United Kingdom, and in respect of which the following sections of the Act are designed to operate. It may be of assistance to stress, in this Note, that a "pre-accession Treaty" does *not* mean a treaty entered into before United Kingdom entry into the Communities on 1st January 1973, but one entered into before the date (22nd January 1972) of the signing of the Treaty of Accession by the United Kingdom and the other countries applying for membership. **[29.1]**

AND ANY OTHER TREATY ENTERED INTO BY ANY OF THE COMMUNITIES . . . OR . . . AS A TREATY ANCILLARY . . . BY THE UNITED KINGDOM

Treaties in either of these two general categories can only be such as are entered into *after* 22nd January 1972 (the date of the signature of the Treaty and Act of Accession). This is because, as regards the first category, "any treaty entered into before the 22nd January 1972 by any of the Communities (with or without any of the member States) . . . " is defined by Sched. 1, Part I, 7, to be a "pre-accesson treaty" and thus is already included in "the Treaties" (in the meaning of the latter phrase used earlier in sub-s. (2)) which are to be "taken with" any other treaty in the two general categories now being considered; and because, as regards the second category, the United Kingdom undertakes by Art. 3 (1) of the Act of Accession "to accede from the date of accession to all other agreements concluded by the original Member States relating to the functioning of the Communities or connected with their activities"—such agreements being clearly those within Sched. 1, Part II, 7, ("any . . . treaty ancillary to any treaty included in this Part of this Schedule by the member States (with or without any other country") and thus also defined as "pre-accession treaties". It may also be conveniently noted at this point that the first part of sub-s. (3), as far as "to be so regarded", is concerned with treaties made *before* 22nd January 1972. (A list of the Community Treaties and related instruments as at 22nd January 1972 is printed as an Appendix to the accession documents, of which it does *not* form part, in Cmnd. 4862—1, pp. 137 *et seq.*)

In the light of the preceding paragraph it becomes clear what types of treaty made *after* 22nd January 1972 may fall into either of the two general categories here being considered. The Treaty between the Coal and Steel Community (*with* the member States) and the Treaty between the Economic Community (*without* the member States), and in both cases, the E.F.T.A. non-candidate countries, exemplify respectively the two types comprised in the first general category, and would seem in principle to require, under the second limb of sub-s. (3) (beginning at "but a treaty entered into by the United Kingdom . . ." to ". . . each House of Parliament"), an affirmative resolution of each House of Parliament. In the second general category, and also within the second limb of sub-s. (3), are "the conventions provided for in Article 220 of the E.E.C. Treaty and . . . the protocols on the interpretation of those conventions by the Court of Justice, signed by the original member States" to which, under Art. 3 (2) of the Act of Accession, the United Kingdom has undertaken to accede "and to this end . . . to enter into negotiations with the original Member States in order to make the necessary adjustments thereto". It is clear that, since negotiations to make the necessary adjustments are to take place, the United Kingdom will not enter into the treaties ancillary to Art. 220 of the E.E.C. Treaty "on terms settled on or before" the 22nd January 1972, so that they are not within the exception ("other than a pre-accession treaty . . .") from the provision of the second limb of sub-s. (3). **[29.2]**

22ND JANUARY 1972

The first four lines of the subsection, as far as "to be so regarded", are concerned with treaties made *before* 22nd January 1972. The remainder of the subsection is concerned with those entered into by the United Kingdom *after* that date. See, under sub-s. (2), AND ANY OTHER TREATY ENTERED INTO BY ANY OF THE COMMUNITIES . . . ETC.

SPECIFIED . . . AS ONE OF THE COMMUNITY TREATIES

Such specification by Order in Council does not, of course, effect any change in the position of the United Kingdom *in international law* in respect of any treaty. The effect is to bring the treaty so specified within the operation of the present Act. As a Community Treaty, a treaty so specified takes effect as a matter of United Kingdom law, in accordance with s. 2 and provisions deriving therefrom. **[29.3]**

SUB-S. (4): TREATY

As here defined, "treaty" has a somewhat wider meaning than is generally accepted for the purposes of public international law, and as in the Vienna Convention on the

Law of Treaties, 1969, (H.M.S.O. Misc. No. 31 Cmnd. 4140). Bearing in mind that the Vienna Convention is restricted to agreements between States only (and excludes (1) agreements between States and other subjects of international law, (2) agreements between such other subjects of international law, and (3) agreements not in written form) the definition it contains in Art. 2, Para. 1 (*a*), may usefully be read together with sub-s. (4). Para. 1 (*a*) of the Convention provides: " 'treaty' means an international agreement concluded between States in written form and governed by international law, whether embodied in a single instrument or in two or more related instruments and whatever its particular designation". Art. 2, para. 2, provides: "The provisions of paragraph 1 regarding the use of terms in the present Convention are without prejudice in the use of those terms or to the meanings which may be given to them in the internal law of any State."

The inclusion by sub-s. (4) of "any protocol or annex to a treaty or international agreement" does not *per se* appear to go outside the definition in Art. 2, para. 1, of the Convention. But the annexes to the Act of Accession and to the Decision (referred to in sub-s. (2) (*a*) and (*b*)) bring within the concept of "treaty" a very wide and numerous range of "related instruments", not only such as Regulations, Decisions, Directives, but also joint declarations, an Exchange of Letters on Monetary Questions, and unilateral declarations, whilst the 30 protocols to the Act of Accession are similarly "related instruments". [**29.4**]

2. General implementation of Treaties

(1) All such rights, powers, liabilities, obligations and restrictions from time to time created or arising by or under the Treaties, and all such remedies and procedures from time to time provided for by or under the Treaties, as in accordance with the Treaties are without further enactment to be given legal effect or used in the United Kingdom shall be recognised and available in law, and be enforced, allowed and followed accordingly; and the expression "enforceable Community right" and similar expressions shall be read as referring to one to which this subsection applies.

(2) Subject to Schedule 2 to this Act, at any time after its passing Her Majesty may by Order in Council, and any designated Minister or department may by regulations, make provision—

(*a*) for the purpose of implementing any Community obligation of the United Kingdom, or enabling any such obligation to be implemented, or of enabling any rights enjoyed or to be enjoyed by the United Kingdom under or by virtue of the Treaties to be exercised; or

(*b*) for the purpose of dealing with matters arising out of or related to any such obligation or rights or the coming into force, or the operation from time to time, of subsection (1) above;

and in the exercise of any statutory power or duty, including any power to give directions or to legislate by means of orders, rules, regulations or other subordinate instrument, the person entrusted with the power or duty may have regard to the objects of the Communities and to any such obligation or rights as aforesaid.

In this subsection "designated Minister or department" means such Minister of the Crown or government department as may from time to time be designated by Order in Council in relation to any matter or for any purpose, but subject to such restrictions or conditions (if any) as may be specified by the Order in Council.

(3) There shall be charged on and issued out of the Consolidated Fund or, if so determined by the Treasury, the National Loans Fund the amounts required to meet any Community obligation to make payments to any of the Communities or member States, or any Community obligation in respect of contributions to the capital or reserves of the European Investment Bank or in

respect of loans to the Bank, or to redeem any notes or obligations issued or created in respect of any such Community obligation; and, except as otherwise provided by or under any enactment,—

(*a*) any other expenses incurred under or by virtue of the Treaties or this Act by any Minister of the Crown or government department may be paid out of moneys provided by Parliament; and

(*b*) any sums received under or by virtue of the Treaties or this Act by any Minister of the Crown or government department, save for such sums as may be required for disbursements permitted by any other enactment, shall be paid into the Consolidated Fund or, if so determined by the Treasury, the National Loans Fund.

(4) The provision that may be made under subsection (2) above includes, subject to Schedule 2 to this Act, any such provision (of any such extent) as might be made by Act of Parliament, and any enactment passed or to be passed, other than one contained in this Part of this Act, shall be construed and have effect subject to the foregoing provisions of this section; but, except as may be provided by any Act passed after this Act, Schedule 2 shall have effect in connection with the powers conferred by this and the following sections of this Act to make Orders in Council and regulations.

(5) The limitations on the legislative power of the Parliament of Northern Ireland which are imposed by section 4 (1) (4) (treaty matters) of the Government of Ireland Act 1920 shall not be construed to prevent that Parliament, on matters otherwise within their powers, from enacting provisions for any of the purposes mentioned in subsection (2) (*a*) and (*b*) above; and the references in that subsection to a Minister of the Crown or government department and to a statutory power or duty shall include a Minister or department of the Government of Northern Ireland and a power or duty arising under or by virtue of an Act of the Parliament of Northern Ireland.

(6) A law passed by the legislature of any of the Channel Islands or of the Isle of Man, or a colonial law (within the meaning of the Colonial Laws Validity Act 1865) passed or made for Gibraltar, if expressed to be passed or made in the implementation of the Treaties and of the obligations of the United Kingdom thereunder, shall not be void or inoperative by reason of any inconsistency with or repugnancy to an Act of Parliament, passed or to be passed, that extends to the Island or Gibraltar or any provision having the force and effect of an Act there (but not including this section), nor by reason of its having some operation outside the Island or Gibraltar; and any such Act or provision that extends to the Island or Gibraltar shall be construed and have effect subject to the provisions of any such law. [30]

GENERAL NOTE

Implementation of the Community Treaties necessitates in the first place the making of *general* provision in respect of the six widely differing matters dealt with respectively in each of the subsections of this section:

(i) making "directly applicable" Community law enforceable in the United Kingdom;

(ii) enabling provision to be made for implementing Community obligations and rights of the United Kingdom;

(iii) payments by the United Kingdom to the Communities and member States and other expenditure and receipts by the United Kingdom;

(iv) the extent of the provision that may be made under (ii), the relationship of (i)–(iii) to other present or future enactments, and the procedural requirements for exercising the powers conferred by this and the following sections of the Act;

(v) enabling the Treaties to be correspondingly implemented in Northern Ireland; and

(vi) adjustment to enable enactments of the Channel Islands or the Isle of Man, or a colonial law made for Gibraltar, to be effective for the purposes of implementing the Treaties, as necessary, in those countries.

SUB-S. (1): GENERAL NOTE

The provisions of the subsection stand in the same relationship to certain elements of Community law, as an effect is related to its cause. The *cause* is the fact that certain elements of Community law are, by that law, considered to be "directly applicable" in member States of the Communities—directly applicable, that is, without any change in their existing form, and without any need for a formal act of legislative recognition by any member State let alone ratification, or re-enactment in national guise. The *effect* of that cause in United Kingdom law, for which the subsection provides, is that such elements of Community law "shall be recognised and available in law, and be enforced, allowed and followed accordingly"—"accordingly", that is, "without further enactment". (As to "directly applicable", see Introduction, *ante*, para. [**16**] and Schedule 1, Part II, under "Community obligation," comment. [**53**].

The elements of Community law which by that effect acquire legal force in United Kingdom law are listed by categories in the opening words of the subsection:—"rights, powers, liabilities, obligations, restrictions, remedies and procedures". It should be noted that there are four ways in which there may come into existence any particular phenomenon of Community law that falls within any one of the first five of the above categories. It may do so because (i) created by, or (ii) created under, or (iii) arising by, or (iv) arising under, the Treaties—so that the coming into existence "from time to time" of such a phenomenon is necessarily provided for by the subsection. Remedies and procedures, which make up the sixth and seventh categories, may come into existence when provided for (i) by or (ii) under, the Treaties, and may thus similarly come into existence "from time to time".

It should be noted that "the coming into force, or the operation from time to time" of the subsection may be the subject of (further) provision made by virtue of sub-s. 2 (b), *infra*. [**30.1**]

ALL SUCH RIGHTS, POWERS, LIABILITIES, ETC.

See the general comment, second paragraph, at the head of this subsection.

FROM TIME TO TIME

See the general note, second paragraph, at the head of this subsection.

THE TREATIES

As defined in s. 1 (2) and (3). See under s. 1 (2) AND ANY OTHER TREATY ENTERED INTO . . . and under s. 1 (4) TREATY.

WITHOUT FURTHER ENACTMENT

By the United Kingdom Parliament.

(The reference is not, nor could it be, to further measures, or further enactment, as a matter of *Community* law; for, in order to be directly applicable in member States, a Community provision must, in the first place, as the European Court has laid down, be "complete and perfect" and require no further measures to make it so).

"Enactment" is not defined in the Act (nor by the Interpretation Act 1889). The expression is used elsewhere in the Act (*e.g.* in s. 2 (4) and in the Heading to Sched. 4 ("Enactments Amended") clearly with the same meaning as that ascribed to it in Stroud's *Judicial Dictionary* (3rd Edition, 1952, p. 950): " 'Enactment' is not the same as the word 'Act'. 'Act' means the whole Act, but an 'enactment' is the Act or a part of it, and a particular section or part of an Act of Parliament may be an 'enactment' (*per* RIDLEY J., *Wakefield Light Railway* v. *Wakefield Corpn*, [1906] 2 K.B. 143: affirmed, [1907] 2 K.B. 256)."

"Enactment" is not infrequently given statutory definition for the particular purposes of the statute in question ("In this Act, unless the context otherwise requires the following expressions have the meaning hereby assigned to them"). Thus, the Local Government Act 1929, s. 134: " 'Enactment' includes any public general, local or private Act and any rule, regulation, byelaw, order, or award made under any Act"; the Gas Undertaking Act 1929, s. 9: " 'Enactment' includes any public general Act, any special Act, and any provisional order confirmed by an Act"; the Local Government Act 1933, s. 305: " 'Enactment' includes any enactment in a provisional order confirmed by Parliament"; the Shops Act 1950, s. 73: " 'Enactment' includes any Act, and any rule, regulation, byelaw, or order made under any Act". In the absence of a definition in the present Act it would seem that 'enactment' should have the meaning defined by RIDLEY J. (*supra*). In the context of the present sub-s. (2) it is clear that the words "without further enactment", following directly the words "in accordance with the Treaties", are descriptive of what is *contemplated in the eyes of Community law*, so that, in that phrase, "enactment" could perhaps be regarded as having a wider meaning than that given it by RIDLEY J. In respect of this aspect of Community law it falls to note that a Regulation (which, by Treaty definition "shall have general application" and "be binding in its entirety and directly applicable in all Member States"—see, for example, E.C. Treaty, Art. 189) frequently needs supplementary measures by individual member States for it to be made effective in the manner contemplated by Community law. Community Regulations, in fact, often contain a specific formula requring member States to take all such necessary measures.

From all the foregoing a twofold result appears to follow: (i) Even if "enactment" is not given a wider meaning than that of RIDLEY J. (*supra*), the effect may not be to exclude, from the operation of sub-s. (1), Community provisions which in the eyes of Community law are directly applicable but require further measures (other than "enactment") under United Kingdom law for their due application, since sub-s. (1) implicitly *obliges* all such necessary supplementary measures to be taken as a matter of United Kingdom law, whilst sub-s. (2) (*b*) ("or the operation from time to time of subsection (1) . . . ") enables the necessary provision for that purpose to be made by Order in Council, or by regulations made by a designated Minister or department; AND (ii) Courts and Tribunals applying sub-s. (1) in respect of any Community instrument (such as a Regulation) may be expected to do so with regard to sub-s. 3 (1), and, "in accordance with the principles laid down by and any relevant decision of the European Court", to determine that, even in the absence of the necessary supplemetary provisions in United Kingdom law, "all such rights, powers, liabilities obligations and restrictions" with which subsection (1) is concerned "shall be . . . enforced, allowed and followed"). (See, for example, the European Court, *Signora Leonisio* v. *Italian Revenue Administration* (Preliminary Ruling on a reference from an Italian municipal court, the Pretura of Lonato): "In its judgment the European Court declared that the Council Regulation was directly applicable and that it created rights for individuals which the national judge was under obligation to uphold. Payments to creditors accruing from such Regulations became due once the prerequsites laid down in the Regulation had been complied with and could not be made subject to rules of implementation other than those for which express provision was made in the Regulation itself." Signora Leonisio, the plaintiff before the Italian Court, had complied with the prerequisites in the Regulation, thus becoming entitled thereunder to payment of a premium, half of which, under the Regulation, was to be provided by the Italian authorities. The Italian Ministry of Agriculture and Forestry, the defendant before the Italian Court, while recognising that the premium was due, had stated that no funds for such payment had as yet been legally appropriated). (The *Times*, 22nd May 1972).

See Introduction *ante* para. [**16**] "directly applicable Community provision"; Sched. 1 Part II, COMMUNITY OBLIGATION, Definition and Note. [**30.2**]

AVAILABLE IN LAW

Cf., in the wider context which is the concern of s. 3 (1), Community law "shall be treated as a question of law", and not of fact. See under WITHOUT FURTHER ENACTMENT *supra*.

ENFORCEABLE COMMUNITY RIGHT

By Sched. 1, Part II, this and similar expressions are to be construed in accordance with the present subsection.

SUB-S. (2): GENERAL NOTE

The primary concern of the subsection (expressed in its first element) is with the implementation of Community obligations *of*, or the enjoyment of Community rights *by, the United Kingdom*. It is not concerned with Community obligations or rights of persons *in* United Kingdom law except in so far as it enables consequential provision to be made in respect of the coming into force or the operation of subsection (1).

The second element of the subsection enables regard to be had to the objects of the Communities and to the Community obligations or rights of the United Kingdom in the excercise of *any* statutory power or duty (not merely one conferred or imposed by the present Act).

SUBJECT TO SCHEDULE 2

See, under sub-s. (4), SUBJECT TO SCHEDULE 2.

It may be noted that the exclusion, by Sched. 2, Para. 1 (1) (*a*), from the powers conferred by the present subsection, of power "to make any provision imposing or increasing taxation", has the result, for example, that United Kingdom obligations to comply with Community Directive(s) or other Community law concerned with Value Added Tax cannot be implemented at all under the present subsection (or the present Act) and necessitate separate enactment by the United Kingdom Parliament.

Obligations of the United Kingdom towards the Communities with respect to other areas of Community law, not expressly implemented by the present Act, such as Freedom of Establishment for example, can and presumably will be implemented by exercise of the powers conferred by the subsection. The same will no doubt be true of Community obligations of the United Kingdom in most areas of Community law requiring implementation, and the powers conferred by the subsection may be exercised "at any time after its (the Act's) passing" as may be necessary—for example, probably, for implementation of E.E.C. Directive 354 concerning units of measurement, which prohibits the use of certain such units after a date (December 1977) more than five years after the passing of the Act. [**30.3**]

AT ANY TIME AFTER ITS PASSING

Thus, even before the entry date, 1st January 1973.

Two orders have so far been made: The Intervention Board for Agricultural Produce Order 1972 (made under s. 6 (2)), and the European Communities (Enforcement of Community Judgements) Order 1972 (made under s. 2 (2)), see Division III, *post.* Regulations under any of ss. 5 (6), (7), 6 (2), (6) in matters of customs or agricultural levies may be required to be made before the entry date, though, in some cases, to take effect on that date and not before. Cf. under sub.-s. (4) POWERS CONFERRED . . .[**30.4**]

BY ORDER IN COUNCIL, MAKE PROVISION

Note Sche. 2, para. 2 (2): "Any statutory instrument containing an Order in Council . . . made in the exercise of a power (conferred by a provision in any section of this Act), if made without a draft having been approved by resolution of each House of Parliament, shall be subject to annulment in pursuance of a resolution of either House." Cf. under sub-s. (4), THE PROVISION, SUBJECT TO SCHEDULE 2, and INCLUDES . . . ANY SUCH PROVISION. [**30.5**]

ANY DESIGNATED MINISTER

That is, designated by Order in Council, as provided by the last five lines of the subsection.

BY REGULATIONS

See, under sub-s. (4) SUBJECT TO SCHEDULE 2, and INCLUDES . . . ANY SUCH PROVISION.

MAKE PROVISION

See, under sub-s. (4), INCLUDES . . . ANY SUCH PROVISION.

COMMUNITY OBLIGATION OF THE UNITED KINGDOM

See, Sched. 1, Part II, COMMUNITY OBLIGATION, Definition and Note.

ANY RIGHTS ENJOYED . . . BY THE UNITED KINGDOM

That is, not any rights enjoyed or to be enjoyed *in* the United Kingdom, which, in so far as they are not provided for by subsection (1) in any event, may be provided for under the last words of (*b*) of this sub-s. (2): "or the coming into force or the operation from time to time, of subsection (1) above".

But it may well be a right *of* the United Kingdom to receive financial aid from the Communities in order to establish, *in* the United Kingdom, a scheme qualifying for such aid. [**30.6**]

ANY SUCH OBLIGATION OR RIGHTS

"Such" relates to s. 2 (2) (*a*): "any Community obligation *of the United Kingdom* . . . any rights enjoyed or to be enjoyed *by the United Kingdom* . . ."

It should be noted that, under s. 2 (2) (*b*), provision may be made by Order in Council or by regulations *either* for implementing the Community obligations or rights of the United Kingdom *referred to in* s. 2 (2) (*a*) (for example, provision complementary to a Community Directive) *or* (by the words immediately following "such obligation or rights") for supplementing directly applicable Community provisions *covered by sub-s.* (1) (for example, for supplementing a Community Regulation, which, although by treaty definition directly applicable, may require further measures to be adopted by a member State in order to take effect therein). See Introduction, Directly Applicable Community Law, *ante*, para [**16**]; (Schedule 1, Part II, COMMUNITY OBLIGATION, note; and cf. s. 6. (4) SUCH PROVISION SUPPLEMENTARY . . .; and Schedule 4B Food 3 (2) (*a*)).

OR THE COMING INTO FORCE, OR THE OPERATION . . . OF SUB-SECTION (1)

Provision by Order in Council, or by Ministerial or departmental regulations, may be consequentially necessary to secure that there shall "be recognised and available in law, and be enforced, allowed and followed", all rights, powers, liabilities, obligations and restrictions as are, under sub-s. (1), "in accordance with the treaties . . . without further enactment to be given legal effect or used in the United Kingdom".

IN THE EXERCISE OF ANY STATUTORY POWER OR DUTY

Any such power or duty, not merely one conferred or imposed by the present Act. The second element of the subsection, referred to in the General Note, *supra*, is contained in the passage beginning with these words and continuing to "such obligation or rights as aforesaid".

INCLUDING ANY POWER TO GIVE DIRECTIONS . . .

Since, by virtue of sub-s. (4), *infra*, "Schedule 2 shall have effect in connction with the powers conferred by this and the following sections of this Act to make Orders in Council and regulations" it would seem, though it is not altogether clear, that the power to give directions conferred by the present sub-s. (2) should fall within Sched. 2, 1 (2): ". . . a power to give directions as to matters of administration is not to be regarded as a power to legislate within the meaning of sub-paragraph (1) (*c*)".

THE PERSON

Or persons, Interpretation Act 1889, s. 1 (1) (*b*), and including, "unless the contrary intention appears", "any body of persons corporate or incorporate", *idem* s. 19.

THE OBJECTS OF THE COMMUNITIES

A broad phrase which would seem to include not only the objects set out in the preambles and introductory Articles of the Treaties of 1951 and 1957 establishing respectively the Coal and Steel Community, the Economic Community and Euratom.

DESIGNATED . . . ANY MATTER . . . ANY PURPOSE

Provided, presumably, that the matter or purpose in within (*a*) or (*b*) of the subsection.

COMMUNITY OBLIGATION TO MAKE PAYMENTS

Under the terms of the Treaty of Accession it becomes the obligation of the United Kingdom to contribute to what are called the Communities' "own resources". These are made up of customs duties (with some exceptions), agricultural levies, and, from 1st January 1975, a proportion equivalent to up to a 1 per cent. rate, of the proceeds of a Value Added Tax to the extent necessary to meet any deficiency. There is, however, to be a phased replacement of existing United Kingdom customs duties by the Community customs system (see s. 5 (1) due to be completed by the end of 1977, and similarly a phased replacement of the United Kingdom agricultural support system by the Community levy system (see s. 6 (7)). The general Community financing system is to become progressively applicable to the United Kingdom and fully applicable for the year 1980 and subsequent years.

The United Kingdom is to make a contribution, equal to those of France and Germany, to the capital of the European Investment Bank, and a proportionate contribution to the Bank's reserves. The United Kingdom is to make an investment in the reserve funds of the Coal and Steel Community of £24 million, to be paid in sterling in three equal annual instalments starting from the date of accession.

The Economic Community Treaty (Arts. 108 and 109) provides for mutual support between member States in the event of a member State encountering balance of payments difficulties. A detailed scheme for medium-term support, if needed, is in existence.

The amounts required for all the above payments are, by the subsection, to be charged on and to issue out of the Consolidated Fund—unless the Treasury determines they shall be charged on and issued out of the National Loans Fund. It appears probable that any medium-term support loans made by virtue of any scheme under Arts. 108 and 109 of the Economic Community Treaty would be charged on the National Loans Fund. [**30.7**]

ANY OTHER EXPENSES . . . MONEYS PROVIDED BY PARLIAMENT

Some of the items at present foreseen are:—

(i) BETWEEN £3 and £4 million annually in respect of some 1,500 additional members of the Civil Service and the associated administrative and accommodation costs;

(ii) Payments across the frontiers, under s. 2, for social security benefits and medical treatment in connection with the movement of persons within the Community, not anticipated to be a significant expense.

(iii) About £1·5 million annually for financing the Sugar Board's operations out of Votes, under s. 7.

(iv) £20 million revenue from customs duties in 1973, deferred once-for-all on introduction of new customs procedures (under s. 4 (1) and Sched. 4) for accepting security on deferring payment of customs duties.

(v) Some contribution from public funds to support schemes that also qualify for financial aid from the Communities.

(vi) There will be savings on the cost of support for agriculture, to be phased out under s. 6 (7). [**30.8**]

ANY SUMS RECEIVED

Under or by virtue of the Treaties—for example:—Community customs duties under s. 5 (3); Community agricultural levies under s. 6 (5); amounts charged for the use of the Sugar Board by a directly applicable Community provision under s. 7 (1).

Under or by virtue of this Act—for example:—Sums received under ss. 5 (3), 6 (5) or 7 (1), as above, prior to the phasing out of the United Kingdom system and its replacement by that of the Community. [**30.9**]

SUB-S. (4): GENERAL NOTE

The subsection is made up of three distinct elements. The first defines the permissible extent or ambit of the provision that may be made by virtue of sub-s. (2) for implementing Community obligations or dealing with matters connected therewith. In the result Orders in Council or Regulations made under sub-s. (2) and subject to Sched. 2 are equated to Acts of Parliament. The second element (beginning immediately after the word "Parliament") provides that all present and future enactments (other than those contained in Part I of the present Act) are to be construed and have effect subject to sub-ss. (1) to (3); but this, it may be noted, is not an entrenched provision. The object is to ensure that Community law shall prevail over United Kingdom law, in accordance with and to the extent required by the Treaties. The third element makes Sched. 2 applicable to the exercise of powers (to make Orders in Council and regulations) conferred by ss. 2–12 inclusive of the Act—except as any later Act may provide.

THE PROVISION

This relates to "make provision" in lines 3 and 4 of sub-s. (2).

SUBJECT TO SCHEDULE 2

The Schedule contains "Provisions as to Subordinate Legislation". Though para. 1 of the Schedule is concerned only with the powers conferred by s. 2 (2), it should be noted that para. 2 applies in respect of "a provision contained in *any* section of this Act" conferring power to make regulations, and requires as a general rule that the power be exercised by statutory instrument. See, under Sched. 2, Note; under sub-s. (2), *supra*, SUBJECT TO SCHEDULE 2.

Cf., *infra*, BUT . . . SCHEDULE 2 SHALL HAVE EFFECT.

INCLUDES . . . ANY SUCH PROVISION (OF ANY SUCH EXTENT) . . . ACT OF PARLIAMENT

The effect of this is that provision made by Order in Council, or regulations made by a "designated" Minister or department, by virtue of sub-s. (2) (*a*) or (*b*), may have the same scope and extent as an Act of Parliament.

The effect is *not*, it seems, to confer the same scope or extent to "the exercise of any statutory power, or duty, etc." in accordance with the second limb of sub-s. (2) (from "and in the exercise of . . ." to ". . . rights as aforesaid"), since that limb is not governed by "make provision" in the third and fourth line of that subsection.

AND ANY ENACTMENT

The second element of the subsection, referred to in the General Note at the head of this subsection, begins with these words.

As to "enactment", see under sub-s. (1) WITHOUT FURTHER ENACTMENT.

PASSED OR TO BE PASSED

This is both retrospective and anticipatory; but it is not an entrenched provision.

OTHER THAN ONE CONTAINED IN THIS PART

But not if contained in Part II; though the effect or practical utility of bringing Part II within the rule of construction that now follows does not appear to amount to very much.

SUBJECT TO THE FOREGOING PROVISIONS OF THIS SECTION

The foregoing provisions are sub-ss. (1) to (3) both inclusive. It seems a little curious that Part II though brought within the rule of construction laid down by the subsection, is not *expressly* required to be construed subject to s. 3. Nor is any "enactment" other than the present Act, "passed or to be passed", expressly required to be construed subject to s. 3.

BUT . . . SCHEDULE 2

The third element of the subsection, referred to in the General Note, *supra*, is comprised in the words from "but" to the end of the subsection.

The general effect of Sched. 2 is to require regulations that are made by virtue of a power conferred by *any* section of the Act to be made by statutory instrument, and to impose certain limitations on the powers conferred by sub-s. (2) of s. 2. But see under Sched. 2, Note. Cf., *supra*, SUBJECT TO SCHEDULE 2.

EXCEPT AS MAY BE PROVIDED BY ANY ACT

The third element of the subsection contains no entrenched provision.

POWERS CONFERRED . . . TO MAKE ORDERS IN COUNCIL AND REGULATIONS

In "this section" such powers are conferred only by sub-s. (2).

In "the following sections of this Act" they are conferred by:—s. 5 (6) (Regulations by the Secretary of State governing reliefs from import duties); s. 5 (7) (Regulations by the Commissioners of Customs and Excise, co-operating with other customs services "for the purpose of implementing Community obligations"); s. 6 (2) (Order(s) in Council as to the constitution and membership of the Intervention Board for Agricultural Produce); s. 6 (2) (Regulations by the Ministers of Agriculture modifying or adding to constitution or powers of any statutory body concerned with agriculture); s. 6 (6) (Regulations by the Commissioners of Customs and Excise prescribing exceptions to or modifications in "the general provisions of the Customs and Excise Act 1952, and ss. 5, 6, 7, 10 and 13 of the Import Duties Act 1958"); s. 10 (2) does *not confer* any power to make regulations, but widens the scope of regulations that may be made under the Restrictive Trade Practices Act 1956, s. 19. [**30.10**]

SUB-S. (5): LIMITATIONS ON THE LEGISLATIVE POWER OF THE PARLIAMENT OF NORTHERN IRELAND

See also, under s. 4 (3) LIMITATIONS ON THE POWERS OF THE PARLIAMENT OF NORTHERN IRELAND (reference to the Northern Ireland (Temporary Provisions) Act, 1972).

SECTION 4 (1) (4) . . . GOVERNMENT OF IRELAND ACT 1920

With regard to the Parliament of Northern Ireland, the 1920 Act provides that it shall not have power to make laws in respect of "Treaties, or any relations with foreign states, or relations with other parts of His Majesty's dominions, or matters involving the contravention of treaties or agreements with foreign states or any part of His Majesty's dominions, or offences connected with any such treaties or relations, or procedure connected with the extradition of criminals under any treaty, or the return of fugitive offenders from or to any part of His Majesty's dominions".

SUB-S. (6): GENERAL NOTE

The purpose of the subsection is to ensure that any law of the Channel Islands or of the Isle of Man, or any colonial law for Gibraltar, "*if expressed to be passed or made in the implementation of the Treaties and of the obligations of the United Kingdom thereunder*" (i) shall prevail over an Act of Parliament—passed or to be passed—that extends to the Island or to Gibraltar and over any provision (other than the present section 2) "having the force and effect of an Act there"; (ii) shall not be void or inoperative "by reason of its having some operation outside the Island or Gibraltar"; and (iii) shall govern the construction and taking effect of any Act of Parliament, or of any provision having the force and effect of an Act, that extends to such Island or to Gibraltar.

The subsection thus provides the constitutional basis for the complete achievement of the latter part of the object expressed in the long Title to the Act:—"to make provision in connection with the enlargement of the European Communities to include the United Kingdom, *together with (for certain purposes) the Channel Islands, the Isle of Man and Gibraltar*".

As to the position of the Islands and Gibraltar in the enlarged Communities see, under THE LONG TITLE, *ante*, paras. [**28.1**] and [**28.2**], THE CHANNEL ISLANDS AND THE ISLE OF MAN and GIBRALTAR. [**30.11**]

3. Decisions on, and proof of, Treaties and Community instruments, etc.

(1) For the purposes of all legal proceedings any question as to the meaning or effect of any of the Treaties, or as to the validity, meaning or effect of any Community instrument, shall be treated as a question of law (and, if not referred to the European Court, be for determination as such in accordance with the principles laid down by and any relevant decision of the European Court).

(2) Judicial notice shall be taken of the Treaties, of the Official Journal of the Communities and of any decision of, or expression of opinion by, the European Court on any such question as aforesaid; and the Official Journal shall be admissible as evidence of any instrument or other act thereby communicated of any of the Communities or of any Community institution.

(3) Evidence of any instrument issued by a Community institution, including any judgment or order of the European Court, or of any document in the custody of a Community institution, or any entry in or extract from such a document, may be given in any legal proceedings by production of a copy certified as a true copy by an official of that institution; and any document purporting to be such a copy shall be received in evidence without proof of the official position or handwriting of the person signing the certificate.

(4) Evidence of any Community instrument may also be given in any legal proceedings—

(*a*) by production of a copy purporting to be printed by the Queen's Printer;

(*b*) where the instrument is in the custody of a government department (including a department of the Government of Northern Ireland), by production of a copy certified on behalf of the department to be a true copy by an officer of the department generally or specially authorised so to do;

and any document purporting to be such a copy as is mentioned in paragraph (*b*) above of an instrument in the custody of a department shall be received in evidence without proof of the official position or handwriting of the person signing the certificate, or of his authority to do so, or of the document being in the custody of the department.

(5) In any legal proceedings in Scotland evidence of any matter given in a manner authorised by this section shall be sufficient evidence of it. [**31**]

GENERAL NOTE

The primary provision of the section, contained in sub-s. (1), requires Community law (whether contained in a Community treaty or in a Community instrument) to be treated in all legal proceedings as a question of *law* (and not as a question of *fact*, as would be the case if Community law were regarded as foreign law). The remaining sub-ss. (2)–(5) make provision, as is consequentially necessary, regarding evidence of Community law.

The section takes effect upon enactment, although recourse to it in legal proceedings prior to the entry date may be unnecessary in practice.

SUB-S. (1) GENERAL NOTE

The subsection contains the primary provision of the section, requiring Community law to be treated in legal proceedings, as *law* and not as *fact*.

ALL LEGAL PROCEEDINGS

The expression is not the strict equivalent of "all judicial proceedings", and must presumably be taken to mean all proceedings to which the rules of natural justice apply.

THE TREATIES

Or, "the Community Treaties", as defined in s. 1(2). See also under s. 1 (2) AND ANY OTHER TREATY ENTERED INTO etc. and Note.

COMMUNITY INSTRUMENT

See Sched. 1, Part II, "Community instrument" and under "Community institution", Definition and Note.

TREATED AS A QUESTION OF LAW

Not as a question of fact, as if the concern were with questions of *foreign* law. For, following the accession to the Communities of the United Kingdom, Community law operates not only *upon* the United Kingdom but *in* the United Kingdom, and all such Community law as is (in the words of s. 2 (1) "in accordance with the Treaties . . . without further enactment to be given legal effect or used in the United Kingdom shall be recognised and available *in law*, and be enforced, allowed and followed accordingly".

REFERRED TO THE EUROPEAN COURT

With the object of promoting the greatest possible uniformity in the application of Community law throughout all the member States, the three Treaties by which the three Communities were originally established conferred jurisdiction on the European Court to give "preliminary rulings" on questions of Community law raised in proceedings before a court or tribunal of a member State. These provisions are more maturely formulated in the two later (1957) Treaties (establishing the Economic Community and Euratom) than they were in the 1952 Coal and Steel Community Treaty.

The identical provisions of Arts. 177 and 150 of the two first named Treaties respectively provide:—

"The Court of Justice shall have jurisdiction to give preliminary rulings concerning:

(*a*) the interpretation of this Treaty;

(*b*) the validity and interpretation of acts of the institutions of the Community;

(*c*) the interpretation of the statutes of bodies established by an act of the Council, where those statutes so provide.

Where such a question is raised before any court or tribunal of a Member State, that court or tribunal may, if it considers that a decision on the question is necessary to enable it to give judgment, request the Court of Justice to give a ruling thereon.

Where any such question is raised in a case pending before a court or tribunal of a Member State, against whose decisions there is no judicial remedy under national law, that court or tribunal shall bring the matter before the Court of Justice."

Art. 41 of the Coal and Steel Community Treaty provides, in French (the only official and authentic language of that Community):—"La Cour est seule compétente pour statuer, à titre préjudiciel, sur la validité des déliberations de la Haute Autorité et du Conseil, dans le cas où un litige porté devant un tribunal national mettrait en cause cette validité." [**31.1**]

PRINCIPLES LAID DOWN BY . . . THE EUROPEAN COURT

There may well be a distinction between, on the one hand, the principles *laid down by* the European Court, and which it has expressly implemented in arriving at particular judgments, and, on the other hand, the principles of a more general nature, particularly of interpretation of the Community Treaties, which the Court manifestly follows as a matter of its own judicial thinking. Thus, in the former group of principles, there falls the Court's declaration that Treaty articles are to be construed not only in the light of the objects clauses that figure early in each Treaty but also in the light of the Preamble to each Treaty. In the latter group falls the principle—or at any rate the habit and custom of the Court to date—of interpreting the Treaties in such a way as to promote the legal development of each Community to the fullest possible extent rather than to impede that development by restrictive interpretation of the Treaties or otherwise. (Much of Community law is in consequence judge made, in a manner not dissimilar from that familiar to common lawyers.)

Uncertainty, in legal proceedings in the United Kingdom, the Channel Islands, the Isle of Man or Gibraltar, whether any such principle of the European Court is to be regarded as having been *laid down* by it, so that by virtue of the subsection it requires to be followed, can the most readily be resolved by a reference from the Court or Tribunal concerned to the European Court itself by virtue of Art. 177 of the E.E.C. Treaty, Art. 150 of the Euratom Treaty or Art. 41 of the Coal and Steel Treaty. [**31.2**]

FOR DETERMINATION . . . IN ACCORDANCE WITH . . . ANY RELEVANT DECISION OF THE EUROPEAN COURT

This provision appears to extend to relevant decisions of the European Court, followed in United Kingdom law, the rule of strict precedent as applied by United Kingdom courts in respect of decisions made originally by those courts.

RELEVANT DECISION . . . OF THE EUROPEAN COURT

"Decision" might be held to include both "Judgment" and "Order", but a decision on "any question as to the meaning or effect of any of the treaties . . ." is more likely to be contained in a judgment. Compare, in sub-s. (2), "decision" and contrast, in sub-s. (3) "judgment or order". As to "European Court", see Sched. 1, Part II, Definition and Note.

The relevancy or otherwise must, in the first place, be for the decision of the Tribunal or Court in which the legal proceedings occur, but it seems the question of relevancy could itself, if need be, be referred by that Tribunal or Court to the European Court (see under IF NOT REFERRED TO THE EUROPEAN COURT, *supra*). [**31.3**]

JUDICIAL NOTICE SHALL BE TAKEN . . .

The corollary, of matters of Community law being treated, not as questions of fact as if matters of foreign law, but as questions of law (sub-s. (1)), is that judicial notice is required to be taken of the sources in which Community law is to be found:—(i) the Treaties (as defined in s. 1 (2)) (and Community secondary legislation made thereunder), (ii) the *Official Journal of the Communities*, and (iii) any relevant decision of, or expression of opinion by, the European Court. (As to the "European Court", see Sched. 1, Part II, Definition and Note.)

The above three sources of Community law thus "prove themselves" in legal proceedings in the United Kingdom. It may also be conveniently noted at this point that any instrument or other act of any Community institution (as to "Community institution", see Sched. 1, Part II, Definition and Note) may be evidenced by the *Official Journal* (under the present subsection) and, alternatively, that any such instrument, or judgment or order of the European Court, or any document in the custody of a Community institution, or any entry in or extract from such a document, may, by virtue of sub-s. (3) *infra*, be evidenced by a certified true copy thereof; and, as a third alternative, any instrument of any Community institution may be evidenced, as provided in sub-s. (4), by production of a copy purporting to be printed by the Queen's Printer, or of a certified true copy if the instrument is in the custody of a government department. Evidence given in any of the above manners is, by sub-s. (5), sufficient evidence in any legal proceedings in Scotland. [**31.4**]

ANY DECISION OF . . . THE EUROPEAN COURT

See, under sub-s. (1), RELEVANT DECISION . . . OF THE EUROPEAN COURT, and, under sub-s. (3) JUDGMENT OR ORDER OF THE EUROPEAN COURT. (As to EUROPEAN COURT, see Schedule 1, Part II, Definition and Note.)

INSTRUMENT OR OTHER ACT . . . OF ANY OF THE COMMUNITIES

This wording seems clearly intended to embrace a different category of acts from the instruments or other acts of a Community *institution*. (The alternative provided by the subsection could be pertinent to an act of a Community; for example, an agreement made by it with a third country, the authority for which rests on an act of an institution, such as a Resolution of the Council.)

OR OTHER ACT . . . OF ANY COMMUNITY INSTITUTION

The wording does not appear to include an act of a Community committee—see Sched. 1, Part II, "Community Institution", Definition and Note.

COMMUNITY INSTITUTION

See Sched. 1, Part II, Definition and Note.

SUB-S. (3): GENERAL COMMENT

The subsection is concerned essentially with what evidence is to be admissible of Community instruments, judgments or orders of the European Court, and documents (or extracts therefrom or entries therein) in the custody of a Community institution. Alternative forms of admissible evidence of Community instruments are provided in both sub-ss. (2) and (4).

EVIDENCE

See under sub-s. (2), JUDICIAL NOTICE SHALL BE TAKEN.

COMMUNITY INSTITUTION.

See Sched. 1, Part II, Definition and Note.

ANY JUDGMENT OR ORDER OF THE EUROPEAN COURT

But, *semble*, not a "report", as to perjury, made under the authority of the European Court, for the purposes of s. 11 (1), *quod vide*.

An "order" is most likely to be an interim or procedural measure of the European Court, though not necessarily so.

ANY LEGAL PROCEEDINGS

As in sub-s. (1), any proceedings to which the rules of natural justice apply.

WITHOUT PROOF OF THE OFFICIAL POSITION OR HANDWRITING

The official of a Community institution, for the purposes of sub-s. (3), is, as to his position or handwriting, treated in the same way as an officer of a United Kingdom government department for the purposes of sub-s. (4). In the case of the latter, however, proof of the officer's authority to sign the certificate, or of the document being in the custody of the department, is also dispensed with (by sub-s. (4)). [**31.5**]

SUB-S. (4): GENERAL COMMENT

The subsection provides for the admissibility of evidence, in forms alternative to those covered by sub-ss. (2) and (3), of Community instruments.

EVIDENCE

See, under sub-s. (2), JUDICIAL NOTICE SHALL BE TAKEN.

COMMUNITY INSTRUMENT.

See Sched. 1, Part II, "Community instrument", Definition and Note; and under s. 11 (1), REPORT . . . UNDER THE AUTHORITY OF THE EUROPEAN COURT.

SUB-S (5): GENERAL COMMENT

The necessity for the provision made by the subsection results from the particularity in Scotland of the concept of "sufficient evidence" (referred to in the last line) and the purpose of the subsection is to ensure that (where this would otherwise *not* be the case) the effect in Scotland of the preceding subsection relating to evidence (that is, sub-ss. (2), (3) and (4)) shall be the same as the effect those subsections produce, without further enactment, elsewhere.

In the absence of sub-s. (5), the effect of sub-ss. (2), (3) and (4) in Scotland would be as follows:—

(i) As to sub-s. (2) there would be no difference; no proof would be required in Scotland of those documents of which the subsection requires judicial notice to be taken.

(ii) But sub-ss. (3) and (4) (concerned with documents not covered by sub-s. (1)) whilst ensuring that a Scottish court would *accept* any Community instrument or decision of the European Court upon the production of a copy thereof—if certified by an official of either the Community Institution concerned or of a Government Department, or alternatively purporting to be printed by the Queen's Printer—would not ensure its *consideration as evidence* by the Scottish court, because without corroboration the document would not constitute "sufficient evidence". A second (supporting) certificate, or the acceptable testimony of an individual as to the document's authenticity, would be necessary. The subsection removes that need for corroboration. [**31.6**]

Part II

Amendment of Law

GENERAL NOTE

The first purpose of Part II is to ensure that as from the entry date there shall be no provision of United Kingdom law—in those relatively few areas of it on which Community law has a bearing—that is incompatible with the due application of Community law by, and in, the United Kingdom (and the Channel Islands, the Isle of Man and Gibraltar). The incompatibilities removed, the second purpose of Part II is to provide that in those same areas of United Kingdom law all necessary amendments are made so as to ensure *positive* compliance with Community obligations in accordance with the Treaties, by, and in, the same countries on and after the entry date.

Positive compliance with Community obligations is required to be in accordance with the Treaties, of which, in regard to the twofold purpose indicated above, the Transitional Measures contained in the Act of Accession have special relevance. These require that in most, though not all, of the same few areas of United Kingdom law in which incompatibilities had first to be removed, Community law shall be substituted for United Kingdom law. But they permit that substitution to be brought about by a phased process, over a number of years rather than all at once on the entry date.

In consequence of this, the repeals and amendments of United Kingdom law effected by Part II (together with Scheds. 3 and 4) are more intricate than would otherwise be the case. Several of the repeals need to be made to take effect, not on the entry date, but on a date, to be appointed, that is related to the phased substitution of Community law for United Kingdom law. Moreover, different dates, rather than a single date, may be required for the repeal of the *same* provision to take effect for *different* purposes.

However, intricacies of this kind are only met with in ss. 5 (Customs Duties), 6 (Agriculture) and 7 (Sugar). In ss. 8 (Cinematograph Films) and 9 (Companies) the substitution of Community law is not phased, but complete and effective on the entry date. S. 10 (Restrictive Trade Practices) is not concerned with substitution at all, but merely with the minor amendments necessary to ensure that United Kingdom law and Community law can operate positively and compatibly *together*, as from the entry date. Ss. 11 (Community offences) and 12 (Furnishing of information to the Communities) make small amendments so as to extend the ambit of United Kingdom law, as from the entry date, so that it may be enforceable, positively, in the furtherance of Community obligations.

The repeals and amendments made by Part II are necessitated either by provisions in the Treaties themselves, or by Community Regulations or Directives. None of these is specifically referred to, let alone incorporated in, the text of any section of the Act, which, it seems, is to be construed without recourse to them, unless that can be shown to be necessary and permissible under the established rules for the interpretation of statutes (see Introduction, *ante*, paras. [**23**] to [**27**]). The one provision as to the construction of Part II that is contained in the Act itself is that of s. 2 (4), in Part I, which provides that "any enactment passed or to be passed, other than one contained in this Part of this Act, shall be construed and have effect subject to the *foregoing* provisions of this section; but . . . Schedule 2 shall have effect in connection with the powers conferred by this and the *following* sections of this Act to make Orders in Council and regulations".

(For convenience of reference, the Community provisions of which account is *directly* taken by Part II are indicated in the Notes. Part II, in interaction with Part I, also makes possible the implementation at the due time and in the due manner of the various Community Regulations and Directives which are covered by the Act of Accession, as follows:—Art. 29 and Annex I, Art. 30 and Annex II, Art. 107 and Annex V, Art. 133 and Annex VII, Art. 150 and Annex X, Art. 152 and Annex XI.) [**31.7**]

4. General provision for repeal and amendment

(1) The enactments mentioned in Schedule 3 to this Act (being enactments that are superseded or to be superseded by reason of Community obligations and of the provision made by this Act in relation thereto or are not compatible with Community obligations) are hereby repealed, to the extent specified in column 3 of the Schedule, with effect from the entry date or other date mentioned in the Schedule; and in the enactments mentioned in Schedule 4 to this Act there shall,

subject to any transitional provision there included, be made the amendments provided for by that Schedule.

(2) Where in any Part of Schedule 3 to this Act it is provided that repeals made by that Part are to take effect from a date appointed by order, the orders shall be made by statutory instrument, and an order may appoint different dates for the repeal of different provisions to take effect, or for the repeal of the same provision to take effect for different purposes; and an order appointing a date for a repeal to take effect may include transitional and other supplementary provisions arising out of that repeal, including provisions adapting the operation of other enactments included for repeal but not yet repealed by that Schedule, and may amend or revoke any such provisions included in a previous order.

(3) Where any of the following sections of this Act, or any paragraph of Schedule 4 to this Act, affects or is construed as one with an Act or Part of an Act similar in purpose to provisions having effect only in Northern Ireland, then—

(*a*) unless otherwise provided by Act of the Parliament of Northern Ireland, the Governor of Northern Ireland may by Order in Council make provision corresponding to any made by the section or paragraph, and amend or revoke any provision so made; and

(*b*) no limitation on the powers of the Parliament of Northern Ireland imposed by the Government of Ireland Act 1920 shall apply in relation to legislation for purposes similar to the purpose of the section or paragraph so as to preclude that Parliament from enacting similar provisions.

(4) Where Schedule 3 or 4 to this Act provides for the repeal or amendment of an enactment that extends or is capable of being extended to any of the Channel Islands or the Isle of Man, the repeal or amendment shall in like manner extend or be capable of being extended thereto. **[32]**

GENERAL NOTE

The main purpose of the section is to effect the repeals and amendments set out respectively in Scheds. 3 and 4, and to make general provision whereunder those repeals and amendments can be made to take effect on different dates (and for different purposes) related to the progressive substitution of Community law for United Kingdom law so far as that is provided for in the following ss. (5–12) of Part II of the Act.

The ancillary purpose is to provide for the extension, or the capability of extension, to Northern Ireland, the Channel Islands and the Isle of Man, of the repeals and amendments listed in Scheds. 3 and 4.

SUB-S. (1): GENERAL NOTE

The subsection effects the *repeal*, as from the *entry date* (1st January 1973), of the enactments listed in Sched. 3, Part IV, and, as from the *appointed date* indicated in Parts I, II and III of Sched. 3, of the enactments listed in those parts. The subsection effects the *amendment*, as from the entry date, of the enactments listed in Sched. 4 (subject to any transitional provision therein).

SUPERSEDED OR TO BE SUPERSEDED

This concerns only Sched. 3. The enactments listed in Part IV thereof are *superseded*. Those listed in Parts I, II and III are *to be superseded*.

COMMUNITY OBLIGATIONS

See Sched. 1, Part II, "Community obligation", Definition and Note.

SUB-S. (2): GENERAL NOTE

A wide range of enactments are repealed by sub-s. (1) and Sched. 3, Parts I, II and III, with effect from a date to be appointed as therein specified. But because of the gradual and progressive manner in which, for the purposes of several sections of the Act, Community law needs to be substituted for United Kingdom law, different dates will frequently be necessary for the repeal of different provisions to take effect, or for the repeal of the same provision to take effect for different purposes. The subsection makes provision for these contingencies not adequately provided for under s. 37 of the Interpretation Act 1889 (the ambit of which does not in any event extend to enabling "an order appointing a date for a repeal to take effect" to "include transitional and other supplementary provisions . . ." as the subsection additionally does). [**32.1**]

MAY INCLUDE TRANSITIONAL AND OTHER SUPPLEMENTARY PROVISIONS
See General Note to the subsection, *supra.*

SUB-S. (3): GENERAL NOTE
The subsection makes provision for the extension to Northern Ireland (which, as part of the United Kingdom, accedes under the Treaties to the European Communities on the entry date) of ss. 5–12 of the Act and, where in point, the amendments effected by any of the paragraphs in Sched. 4.

CONSTRUED AS ONE WITH . . .
S. 7 "shall be construed as one with the Sugar Act, 1956" (s. 7 (4)).
S. 8 "shall be construed as one with the Films Act, 1960" (s. 8 (5)).
S. 9 "shall be construed as one with the Companies Act, 1948" (s. 9 (8)).

The Films Act 1960 (by s. 52 (4)), and the Companies Act, 1948 (by s. 461), do not extend to Northern Ireland. The Companies Act (Northern Ireland) 1960 as amended by the Companies Act (Northern Ireland) 1963 is the only one containing "provisions having effect only in Northern Ireland" to which the subsection can apply. There are no provisions having effect only in Northern Ireland to which the Films Act 1960 is "similar in purpose".

The Sugar Act 1956 extends to Northern Ireland (by s. 36 (2)) "with the exception of ss. 7–16" (which sections are among those repealed, with effect from the appointed date by s. 4 (1) and Sched. 3, Part II). [**32.2**]

THE GOVERNOR OF NORTHERN IRELAND
By the Northern Ireland (Temporary Provisions) Act 1972 (c. 22), s. 1 (1)), "So long as this section has effect, the Secretary of State (for Northern Ireland) shall act as chief executive officer as respects Irish services instead of the Governor of Northern Ireland.'

LIMITATION ON THE POWERS OF THE PARLIAMENT OF NORTHERN IRELAND
By the Northern Ireland (Temporary Provisions) Act 1972 (c. 22) s. 1 (3) (first paragraph), "So long as this section has effect, the Parliament of Northern Ireland shall stand prorogued (and no writ need be issued to fill any vacancy); and Her Majesty shall have power by Order in Council to make laws for any purpose for which the Parliament of Northern Ireland has power to make laws, and may by any such Order in Council confer powers on the Secretary of State (for Northern Ireland) or any other Minister or department of the Government of the United Kingdom". [**32.3**]

SUB-S. (4): GENERAL NOTE
Similar in purpose to sub-s. (3) which has regard only to Northern Ireland, the subsection provides for the extension, or the capability of extension, to the Channel Islands and to the Isle of Man of the repeals and amendments, listed in Scheds. 3 and 4, of any enactment that itself so extends or is capable of being extended. [**32.4**]

5. Customs duties

(1) Subject to subsection (2) below, on and after the relevant date there shall be charged, levied, collected and paid on goods imported into the United Kingdom such Community customs duty, if any, as is for the time being applicable in accordance with the Treaties or, if the goods are not within the common customs tariff of the Economic Community and the duties chargeable are not otherwise fixed by any directly applicable Community provision, such duty of customs, if any, as the Treasury, on the recommendation of the Secretary of State, may by order specify.

For this purpose "the relevant date", in relation to any goods, is the date on and after which the duties of customs that may be charged thereon are no longer affected under the Treaties by any temporary provision made on or with reference to the accession of the United Kingdom to the Communities.

(2) Where as regards goods imported into the United Kingdom provision may, in accordance with the Treaties, be made in derogation of the common customs tariff or of the exclusion of customs duties as between member States, the Treasury may by order make such provision as to the customs duties chargeable on the goods, or as to exempting the goods from any customs duty, as the Treasury may on the recommendation of the Secretary of State determine.

(3) The customs duties charged in accordance with subsections (1) and (2) above shall be deemed for the purposes of any enactment to be import duties charged under the Import Duties Act 1958 (but references to the enactments relating to customs generally shall not by reason thereof be treated as including that Act); and, subject to any amendment made by this Act, section 13 of that Act shall apply to orders under subsection (1) or (2) above as if they were orders under that Act.

(4) Except as otherwise provided by or under this Act or any later enactment, the law in force at the passing of this Act in relation to customs duties shall continue to apply, notwithstanding that any duties are imposed for the benefit of the Communities, as if the revenue from duties so imposed remained part of the revenues of the Crown.

(5) So long as section 1 of the Import Duties Act 1958 remains in force, that Act shall have effect subject to the following modifications:—

(*a*) the power under section 1 to impose duties shall include power to impose duties with a view to securing compliance with any Community obligation;

(*b*) orders under section 1 may, in relation to goods of the same description, make different provision by reference to the use to be made of the goods or to other matters not ascertainable from an examination of the goods;

(*c*) the powers exercisable by virtue of section 2 (1) in relation to goods qualifying for Commonwealth preference shall include power to distinguish in any respect between different parts of the Commonwealth preference area;

(*d*) the powers exercisable by virtue of section 5 (1) and (4) together with paragraph 8 of Schedule 3 shall, as regards relief provided for by or under the Treaties or for conformity with any Community obligation, extend to any customs duties.

(6) As regards reliefs from import duties, the Secretary of State may by regulations make such further provision as appears to him to be expedient having regard to the practices adopted or to be adopted in other member States, whether by law or administrative action and whether or not for conformity with Community obligations; and any such regulations may amend or repeal accordingly any of the provisions of Part II of the Import Duties Act 1958 or section 1 of the Finance Act 1966, as modified by this Act.

(7) For the purpose of implementing Community obligations the Commissioners of Customs and Excise shall co-operate with other customs services on matters of mutual concern, and (without prejudice to the foregoing) may for that purpose—

(*a*) give effect, in accordance with such arrangements as they may direct or by regulations prescribe, to any Community requirement or practice as to the movement of goods between countries, including any rules requiring payment to be made in connection with the exportation of goods to compensate for any relief from customs duty allowed or to be allowed (and may recover any such payment as if it were an amount of customs duty unpaid); and

(*b*) give effect to any reciprocal arrangements made between member States (with or without other countries or territories) for securing, by the exchange of information or otherwise, the due administration of their customs laws and the prevention or detection of fraud or evasion.

(8) Where on the exportation of any goods from the United Kingdom there has been furnished for the purpose of any Community requirement or practice any certificate or other evidence as to the origin of those goods, or as to payments made or relief from duty allowed in any country or territory, then for the purpose of verifying or investigating that certificate or evidence, the Commissioners or an officer may require the exporter, or any other person appearing to the Commissioners or officer to have been concerned in any way with the goods, or with any goods from which, directly or indirectly, they have been produced or manufactured, or to have been concerned with the obtaining or furnishing of the certificate or evidence,—

(*a*) to furnish such information, in such form and within such time, as the Commissioners or officer may specify in the requirement; or

(*b*) to produce for inspection, and to allow the taking of copies or extracts from, such invoices, bills of lading, books or documents as may be so specified;

and any person who, without reasonable cause, fails to comply with a requirement under this subsection shall be liable to a penalty of £50.

(9) Subsections (7) and (8) above shall have effect as if contained in the Customs and Excise Act 1952. **[33]**

GENERAL NOTE

The main purpose of the section (apparent from sub-ss. (1) and (2)) is to provide for the progressive, and ultimately complete, substitution of Community customs duties for United Kingdom import duties, in respect of goods imported into the United Kingdom (or, for most purposes, the Channel Islands or the Isle of Man—see comment under the Long Title) and also to provide for the steps in that progressive, essentially arithmetical, substitution, to be synchronised with the progressive substitution of Community jurisdiction in respect of customs duties for the jurisdiction of the United Kingdm.

When the substitution is complete, there will be no customs duties in the United Kingdom on imports from member States of the Communities, and, on imports from non-member States, the duties applied by the United Kingdom will be identical with the duties applied in common by all member States to such imports, in accordance with Community law.

But the substitution requires to be made to progress towards ultimate completion—rather than to be effected completely on enactment—in accordance with the Transitional Measures contained in the Act of Accession. These provide, *first*, for the progressive abolition of customs duties on imports between the Community, as originally constituted with six member States, and the new member States, as well as on imports between the new member States themselves—by successive percentage reductions of the "basic duty", this being the rate actually applied by the new member States on 1st January 1972—in accordance with a time-table covering the period from the 1st April 1973 to the end of 1977. The Transitional Measures provide, *secondly*, for the progressive adjustment—in accordance with a time-table covering the period 1st January 1974 to 1st July 1977—of the tariffs applicable by the new member States to non-member countries, until the point is reached where these tariffs become identical with those of the common customs tariff of the Economic Community, or with those of the unified tariff of the Coal and Steel Community, or with the tariffs applied under the Economic Community's various preferential Agreements (*vis-à-vis* Spain and Turkey, for example), as the case may be.

Within the above time-tables, the date of final abolition of the "basic duty" or of complete identification with the Communities' tariffs applicable to non-member countries, varies according to the category of goods to which the "basic duty" or the tariff formerly applied. The section calls each such date "the relevant date". The "relevant date" is, of course, the date on which customs duty on the category of goods in question is, in the words of the section, "no longer affected under the Treaties by any temporary provision made on or with reference to the accession of the United Kingdom to the Communities", and the date from which *Community* customs duties, in relation to non-member countries of the Communities, are charged by virtue of Community jurisdiction on imports into the United Kingdom.

The section provides (in sub-ss. (3) to (7)) the mechanics for the achievement of the above purpose by recourse—broadly speaking—to the Import Duties Act 1958 (for the charging of, or relief from, import duties during the operation of the Transitional Measures) and by recourse to the Customs and Excise Act 1952 (for what that Act describes as "the collecting and accounting for, and otherwise managing, the revenues of customs . . ."). The consequential repeal (by s. 4 (1) and Sched. 3) when its purpose, as above, has been served, of certain parts of the Import Duties Act 1958 (mainly its charging provisions) is to take effect on a date, appointed by the Secretary of State, which, clearly, cannot be prior to the final "relevant date". Much of the 1958 Act, and also of the Customs and Excise Act 1952 is amended (by s. 4 (1) and Sched. 4) to make provision for these new tasks that have to be carried out.

An ancillary purpose of the section is to make provision (by sub-s. (8)) as to certificates or other evidence of origin, or as to payments made or relief from duty allowed in any country, on the exportation of goods from the United Kingdom.

(Community instruments concerned with Customs Legislation referred to in Art. 29 of the Act of Accession are listed in Annex I thereto (Cmnd. 4862—II, pp. 5–21): only one such instrument, referred to in Art. 30 of the Act of Accession, is contained in Annex II thereto (Cmnd. 4862—II, at p. 135). (See also Annex VIII, *idem* at pp. 147–148; Annex XI, *idem* at p. 165. [**33.1**]

SUB-S. (1): GENERAL NOTE

The main purposes of the subsection are to provide for the progressive transfer to the Community of jurisdiction in respect of the duties applied by the United Kingdom to non-member countries of the Economic Community and to put beyond any doubt the legal obligation to pay the duties fixed by the Community. Such customs duties fall to be uniformly administered by all member States in relation to non-member countries only.

The subsection takes effect on and after "the relevant date" in relation to any category of goods, and is not dependent for this purpose on either the date of enactment or the "entry date".

The further purpose of the subsection is to provide for specification, by the order of the Treasury, of the duty of customs on goods imported into the United Kingdom on and after "the relevant date" which are "within the common customs tariff of the Economic Community" and on which "the duties chargeable are not otherwise fixed by any directly applicable Community provision". [**33.2**]

SUBJECT TO SUBSECTION (2)

In addition to the two alternatives for which provision is made in sub-s. (1) (namely goods subject, on and after the relevant date, to directly applicable Community customs duty, and goods not so subject) there are two further alternatives, namely, goods, although so subject, and goods excluded by Community law from customs duties as between member States, which may in either case, in accordance with the Treaties, be the subject of a provision in derogation of the Community customs arrangements otherwise applicable to them. Sub-s. (2) makes provision for this derogation. [**33.3**]

ON AND AFTER THE RELEVANT DATE

The relevant date is defined lower down in the subsection. In that definition the words "any temporary provision made on or with reference to the accession of the United Kingdom to the Communities" refer to the "Transitional Measures" in Arts. 31–41 (or other Articles such as 47, 59 and 60, which in the main refer back to Articles 31–39) of the Act of Accession, under which United Kingdom customs duties on imports are progressively replaced by nil duties or Community customs duties in accordance with the timetables therein set out. Since the replacement is subject to different time-tables, the relevant date will not be the same for all categories of goods and is therefore expressed to be "in relation to any goods". (Cf. under s. 6 (7) PRODUCE OF ANY DESCRIPTION.) The final relevant date is the end of 1977, from which date the new member States are required by Art. 39 of the Act of Accession to "apply in full the Common Customs Tariff and the E.C.S.C. unified tariff". [**33.4**]

CHARGED LEVIED COLLECTED PAID

These words take up the traditional formula of United Kingdom law relating to customs duties. The expression "charged" is essential because the Regulations establishing the common customs tariff merely fix (see "fixed" five lines lower down in the subsection) the rates of duty payable without imposing, in terms, a charge for their payment (though they might possibly be held to do so by necessary construction or material implication). (Community agricultural levies, by contrast, are directly charged; see ss. 6 (5) and 7 (1)).

The Community customs duties charged under sub-s. (1) are (by sub-s. (3)) "deemed for the purposes of any enactment to be import duties charged under the Import Duties Act 1958". The charging provisions of that Act are repealed by s. 4 (1) and Sched. 3, Part 1, with "effect from such date as the Secretary of State may by order appoint". It follows that the date so appointed will not be earlier than the (latest) "relevant date". [**33.5**]

SUCH COMMUNITY CUSTOMS DUTY

A Community customs duty is one "fixed . . . by directly applicable Community provision . . ." (Sched. 1, Part II, Definition and Note.) By virtue of sub-s. (3), Community customs duties "shall be deemed for the purposes of any enactment to be import duties charged under the Import Duties Act 1958". Much of that Act is repealed with "effect from such date as the Secretary of State may by order appoint" in order to allow Community law on that date to take its place, after the "relevant date" (see RELEVANT DATE, *infra*). But, by virtue of sub-s. (5), "so long as section 1 of the Import Duties Act 1958 remains in force . . . (*a*) the power under section 1 to impose duties shall include power to impose duties with a view to securing compliance with any Community obligation". Such compliance is in point in the present subsection. [**33.6**]

NOT WITHIN THE COMMON CUSTOMS TARIFF . . .

Goods to which the unified tariff of the Coal and Steel Community applies are not within the Common Customs Tariff of the Economic Community. It is provided in the Act of Accession, Art. 31, that: "For the purposes of this Act, 'E.C.S.C. unified tariff' means the customs nomenclature and the customs duties for the products in Annex 1 to the E.C.S.C. Treaty, other than coal." Annex 1 to the E.C.S.C. Treaty is headed "Definition of the Expressions 'Coal' and 'Steel' " and lists these products under two main sub-headings: 'Fuels' and 'Iron and Steel'.

AND . . . NOT OTHERWISE FIXED BY ANY DIRECTLY APPLICABLE COMMUNITY PROVISION

The unified tariff of the Coal and Steel Community is *not* a directly applicable Community provision. As to "fixed" see CHARGED LEVIED COLLECTED PAID, *supra*. As to "directly applicable Community provision" see Sched. 1, Part II, "Community obligation", Definition and Note, also Introduction *ante*, para. [**16**] *et seq.*

THE SECRETARY OF STATE

The Secretary of State for Trade and Industry. In the Import Duties Act 1958 (which is applicable to the present subsection as provided in sub-s. (3)) the words "the Secretary of State" are substituted throughout for "the Board of Trade" or "the Board", and in Part II and Sched. 3 for "the Treasury", by the amendment effected by s. 4 (1) and Sched. 4 A (i), 1 (1) of the present Act. Cf. under s. 6 (5) References to the Secretary of State. The Interpretation Act, 1889 s. 12 (3) provides: "The expression 'Secretary of State' shall mean one of Her Majesty's Principal Secretaries of State for the time being."

MAY BY ORDER SPECIFY

The Treasury may not make such an order unless the goods are *both* "not within the common customs tariff of the Economic Community *and* the duties chargeable thereon are "not otherwise fixed by any directly applicable Community provision", as to both of which conditions see *supra*. (The recommendation of the Secretary of State, as under the Import Duties Act 1958, s. 1, is also necessary).

By virtue of sub-s. (3), s. 13 of the Import Duties Act 1958 (as amended by the present Act, s. 4 (1) and Sched. 4A (i), 1(1) (*a*), (*b*) and (5)) applies to any such order as if it were an order under the 1958 Act. Consequently, the power to make orders is exercisable by statutory instrument, and includes "power to vary or revoke any order made in the exercise of that power". S. 13 of the 1958 Act, as amended, takes effect upon enactment of the present Act. The text is at para [**33.12**] *post.* [**33.7**]

IN RELATION TO ANY GOODS

See under ON AND AFTER THE RELEVANT DATE, *supra*.

TEMPORARY PROVISION

This is a reference to the Transitional Measures relating to the Free Movement of Goods (and, under that head, the Tariff Provisions) provided for in or under the Act of Accession (Arts. 31–41). See also ON AND AFTER THE RELEVANT DATE, *supra*.

SUB-S. (2): GENERAL NOTE

The subsection enables the Treasury to make provision as to the customs duty chargeable, or as to the exemption from customs duty, on goods imported into the United Kingdom, where, in accordance with the Treaties, it is permissible for a single member State to act "in derogation of" the otherwise applicable Community provisions. There are two aspects of the normally applicable Community provisions; these are, in the words of Art. 9 of the Economic Community Treaty, (i) "the prohibition between member States of customs duties on imports and exports and of all charges having equivalent effect", and (ii) "the adoption of a common customs tariff in their relations with third countries". The subsection provides for "derogation" from either of these alternatively. Some recourse has been made to both in the practice of the original Community of six member States. Derogation is not expressed to apply to goods covered by the unified tariff of the Coal and Steel Community, except in respect of "the exclusion of customs duties as between member states." [**33.8**]

IN ACCORDANCE WITH THE TREATIES

"The Treaties" include the Treaty (and Act) of Accession (see s. 1 (2)), so that these words imply that the subsection cannot take effect until the entry date.

IN DEROGATION

Derogation is of Community law providing (in Art. 9 of the E.C. Treaty) (i) the prohibition between member States of customs duties on imports and exports and of all charges having equivalent effect, and (ii) the adoption of a common customs tariff in their relations with third countries. In providing for "derogation of the common customs tariff the subsection must presumably be referring to the common customs tariff *of the Economic Community* (as in sub-s. (1)) and therefore excludes derogation of the unified tariff of the Coal and Steel Community. The possibility of derogation "of the common customs tariff or of the exclusion of customs duties as between member States"—as the subsection puts it—derives from the E.C. Treaty and figures in E.E.C. Council Regulation 950 of 1968. [**33.9**]

BY ORDER

The power to make orders is exercisable by statutory instrument (sub-s. (3)) and the Import Duties Act 1958, s. 13, as amended by the present Act (see Sched. 4A (i), 1 (1) (*a*) and (5) and text of amended section, unser sub-s. (3) SECTION 13)).

THE CUSTOMS DUTY CHARGEABLE

Such is a United Kingdom customs duty, not a Community customs duty, which is the concern of sub-s. (1). But like the latter, by virtue of sub-s. (3), United Kingdom customs duties charged under the present subsection "shall be deemed for the purposes of any enactment to be import duties charged under the Import Duties Act 1958". As to the repeal of that Act, see SUCH COMMUNITY CUSTOMS DUTY under sub-s. (1), *supra*, and DUTIES CHARGED UNDER THE IMPORT DUTIES ACT 1958 under sub-s. (3), *infra*.

SUB-S. (3): GENERAL NOTE

The subsection provides that Community customs duties and United Kingdom customs duties, charged in accordance with sub-s. (1) and (2) respectively, shall be deemed to be import duties charged under the Import Duties Act 1958, and that s. 13 of that Act, as amended, shall apply to orders made under either of those subsections.

The purpose is to extend various reliefs afforded under the Import Duties Act 1958 (*e.g.*, s. 7), from duties charged under that Act, to duties charged under sub-s. (1) or (2) of the present Act. Without the provision made by sub-s. (3) the reliefs would cease to be available once duties stopped being charged under the 1958 Act. (On and after the relevant date Community customs duties become chargeable as such, by virtue of sub-s. (1), and the need for them to be deemed to be something else is in fact removed, but the power of charging under the Import Duties Act 1958 remains until the repeal of the relevant part of that Act takes effect on the appointed day. Prior to that day, as each relevant date is reached and Community customs duties become directly applicable in respect of a given category of goods, no order under the Import Duties Act imposing a charge requires to be made.) [**33.10**]

DUTIES CHARGED UNDER THE IMPORT DUTIES ACT 1958

The Import Duties Act 1958 (as already amended by the Finance Act 1969 s. 54 (2) (*b*) and (*c*), in respect of minor matters in s. 6) is amended, primarily in respect of Import Duty Reliefs and also in respect of s. 13, by s. 4 (1) and Sched. 4A (1) of the present Act, with effect upon its enactment. By s. 4 (1) and Sched. 3, Part I, the whole Import Duties Act 1958 is repealed, except for s. 4 and much of Part II (ss. 5–10), "Relief from Import Duties", with "effect from such date as the Secretary of State may by order appoint". The order is to be made by statutory instrument (s. 4 (2)). As from that appointed date the power to charge import duty, conferred by s. 1, will no longer exist under the Import Duties Act, but s. 13 ("Provisions as to orders and regulations") will remain in force—and by virtue of the present subsection will "apply to orders under sub-s. (1) or (2) above as if they were orders under that Act". Were there not the present power of the Treasury to charge import duties under the 1958 Act, the task of the Commissioners of Customs and Excise under the Customs and Excise Act 1952 could not be fulfilled in respect of such import duties. (The 1952 Act, s. 1 (2), provides: "The Commissioners shall, subject to the general control of the Treasury, be charged with the duty of collecting and accounting for, and otherwise managing, the revenues of customs and excise.") When the power to charge under the 1958 Act ceases on the appointed date to exist, the duty of the Commissioners will fall to be fulfilled in respect of the charge, on imported goods, resulting from Community customs duties as a matter of a "directly applicable Community provision" (Sched. 1, Part II, Other Definitions, "Community customs duty" and Note). The Commissioners' duty will fall to be fulfilled in this way by virtue of sub-s. (4) which provides that "the law in force at the passing of this Act in relation to customs duties shall continue to apply, notwithstanding that any duties are imposed for the benefit of the Communities". [**33.11**]

REFERENCES TO THE ENACTMENTS RELATING TO CUSTOMS GENERALLY

Such references are made to exclude the Import Duties Act 1958 which, as to its charging provisions, is repealed with effect from the appointed date (see DUTIES CHARGED etc. immediately, *supra*). The need for it to be excluded is exemplified by the reference in sub-s. (4) to "the law . . . in relation to customs duties" continuing to apply.

BY REASON THEREOF

By reason of the customs duties charged in accordance with sub-ss. (1) and (2) being deemed to be import duties under the 1958 Act.

SECTION 13

S. 13 (2) requires orders under sub-ss. (1) and (2) to be made by statutory instrument, and by s. 13 (4) where such an order "imposes or increases any duty of customs, or restricts any relief from duty under section five of this Act, unless the order states that it does not do so otherwise than in pursuance of a Community obligation, the statutory instrument shall be laid before the Commons House of Parliament" for approval by resolution. The quoted words in s. 13 (4) between "duty of customs" and "the statutory, instrument" result from the amendment made by s. 4 (1) and Sched. 4A (i) 1 (5), and are necessary because where the imposition, increase or restriction is in pursuance of a Community obligation, the fulfilment of that obligation is incumbent in any event on the United Kingdom.

The Import Duties Act 1958, s. 13, as amended by the Finance Act 1969 and the present Act provides:—

"(1) Any power to make orders which is conferred by this Act shall include power to revoke or vary any order made in the exercise of that power.

(2) Any power of the Treasury or the Secretary of State to make orders or regulations under this Act shall be exercisable by statutory instrument.

(3) In any case not falling within the next following subsection, any statutory instrument containing any such order or regulations shall be subject to annulment in pursuance of a resolution of the Commons House of Parliament.

(4) Where an order under this Act imposes or increases any duty of customs, or restricts any relief from duty under section five of this Act, *unless the order states that it does not do so otherwise than in pursuance of a Community obligation*, the statutory instrument shall be laid before the Commons House

of Parliament after being made, and the order shall cease to have effect at the end of twenty-eight days after that on which it is made (but without prejudice to anything previously done under the order or to the making of a new order) unless at some time before the end of those twenty-eight days the order is approved by resolution of that House. In reckoning for the purposes of this subsection any period of twenty-eight days, no account shall be taken of any time during which Parliament is dissolved or prorogued or during which the Commons House is adjourned for more than four days.

(5) Where an order has the effect of altering the rate of duty on any goods in such a way that the new rate is not directly comparable with the old, it shall not be treated for the purposes of subsection (4) of this section as increasing the duty on those goods if it declares the opinion of the Treasury to be that, in the circumstances existing at the date of the order, the alteration is not calculated to raise the general level of duty on the goods.

(6) Subsection (1) of section eleven of the Customs Duties (Dumping and Subsidies) Act, 1957, shall have effect (except as respects orders laid before the House of Commons before the date of the passing of this Act) as if the references to subsections (1) to (4) of section nineteen of the Import Duties Act, 1932, and to orders under the Import Duties Act, 1932, were references to subsections (3) to (5) of this section and to orders of the Treasury under this Act." **[33.12]**

SUB-S. (4): GENERAL NOTE

The subsection provides for the continuance of existing law relating to customs duties and provides for customs duties imposed for the benefit of the Communities to be dealt with as if the revenue therefrom remained part of the revenues of the Crown. The aim is not only to make applicable to such customs duties the existing law as to collecting, accounting for and otherwise managing, customs revenues, but to ensure the enforcement of arrangements, made for these purposes, by bringing them within the range of offences under the existing law and providing for the application thereto of the procedures and penalties of United Kingdom law. (So that, *for example*, ss. 9 (1) and 45 of the Customs and Excise Act 1952, concerning respectively offences by Commissioners or officers and improper importation of goods, apply in respect of customs duties imposed for the benefit of the Communities.) **[33.13]**

EXCEPT AS OTHERWISE PROVIDED BY OR UNDER THIS ACT

The Act, by s. 4 (1), and Sched. 3, Part I, *repeals* the whole of the Customs Duties (Dumping and Subsidies) Act 1969, a consolidation Act: by Sched. 3, Part II, *repeals* the provisions in the Sugar Act 1956 regarding the administrative expenses under that Act of the Commissioners of Customs and Excise; by Sched. 3, Part IV, *repeals* Sched. 6 (the so-called "valuation schedule") of the Customs and Excise Act 1952, except for cases in which the value of goods falls to be determined as at a time before the entry date.

The Act, by s. 4 (1) and Sched. 4A (ii) 2, *amends* some provisions of the Customs and Excise Act 1952. These amendments are annotated under Sched. 4, para. **[61]** *et seq.*, *post.* **[33.14]**

AS IF THE REVENUE FROM DUTIES . . . REMAINED PART OF THE REVENUES OF THE CROWN

If it were not treated as revenue of the Crown, the Commissioners of Customs and Excise would not have, in respect of it, the duty under the Customs and Excise Act 1952, s. 1 (2), "of collecting and accounting for, and otherwise managing, the revenues of customs . . ."; nor would the provisions of ss. 301 to 305 ("General Offences") of that Act apply and there would be no sanctions to enforce compliance with the Commissioners' lawful requirements under the Act (see general comment at the head of this subsection, and cf. s. 6 (5), para. **[34.14]**, *post* . . .). **[33.15]**

SUB-S. (5): GENERAL NOTE

The purpose of sub-s. (5) is to make the modifications to ss. 1, 2 (1), 5 (1) and (4) of the Import Duties Act 1958 necessary for their application in relation to Community obligations. (S. 1 of the Import Duties Act 1958 (containing its charging provisions) is repealed by s. 4 (1) and Sched. 3, Part I, with "effect from such date as the Secretary of State may by order appoint", but is in the meantime essential for the charging of Community customs duties (under sub-s. (1) (whether "directly applicable" or not) deemed (by virtue of sub-s. (3)) to be import duties under the Import Duties Act 1958.)

SO LONG AS SECTION I OF THE IMPORT DUTIES ACT REMAINS IN FORCE

The section is repealed by s. 4 (1) and Sched. 3, Part I, with "effect from such date as the Secretary of State may by order appoint" (the order being made by statutory instrument, s. 4 (2)). See, under sub-s. (3), DUTIES CHARGED UNDER THE IMPORT DUTIES ACT 1958.

THE FOLLOWING MODIFICATIONS

As to COMMUNITY OBLIGATION, see Sched. 1, Part II, Definition and Note. The Community obligation relevant to modification (*a*) arises under the Treaty and Act of Accession (specifically, the Transitional measures therein contained) under which Community customs duties must by progressive stages be substituted for United Kingdom import duties. (This progressive substitution is provided for in sub-s. (1) by reference to the relevant date on which, in relation to any category of goods, the duties chargeable thereon "are no longer affected by any temporary provision made on or with reference to the accession of the United Kingdom to the Communities".)

The objects of s. 5 (5) (*a*) to (*d*) are described in the paragraphs which now follow.

Modification (*a*) extends the power under s. 1 of the Import Duties Act 1958 to embrace the imposition of duties "with a view to securing compliance with . . . (the) . . . Community obligation" to effect the above substitution. Without the modification the power to comply would not exist, for the section makes possible only the protection of United Kingdom producers or the creation of a Commonwealth Preference.

The object of modification (*b*) is twofold: to enable different provision to be made in regard to

(i) what is conveniently referred to as "the end use" of imported goods. (For example, on imported apples intended for the making of cider there may be relief from duty under the Third Schedule, para. 6, of the 1958 Act; but on other imported apples ("goods of the same description") not so intended, no similar relief is available. As a result of the modification, provision may now be made to ensure that imported cider apples are in fact put to their intended end use.)

(ii) For example, recourse to experts, to determine whether imported animals "of the same description" (horse, dog etc.) differ by being thoroughbred or not.

The modification is complemented by amendment of s. 255 of the Customs and Excise Act 1952 (for text of which see under Sched. 4, *post*, para. [**62**]).

S. 2 (1) of the Import Duties Act 1958 requires Commonwealth Preference to be regarded as indivisible, whilst the Act of Accession requires it to be divided (goods from Canada, for instance, will become dutiable, whilst goods from Nigeria will not). The extension of the s. 2 (1) powers to include power to distinguish between different parts of the Commonwealth preference area is thus necessary during the transitional period following the entry date, because of the different relationships with the Communities of different parts of the Commonwealth area (whether due to an Association Agreement with the Communities, or otherwise) and of the provisions relating thereto contained in the Transitional Measures of the Act of Accession (see especially Art. 109 (3), Annex VI and Protocol No. 22).

S. 2 (1) of the Import Duties Act 1958 provides: "Orders under section one of this Act may provide that the import duty imposed on goods of any description shall not be chargeable on goods qualifying for Commonwealth preference or shall be chargeable on them at a preferential rate; and the power conferred by that section to impose import duties with a view to affording protection to goods produced in the United Kingdom shall include power to impose import duties with a view to affording preference to goods qualifying for Commonwealth preference." The section is repealed with effect from the appointed date—Sched. 3, Part I.

Import duties under the Import Duties Act 1958 (s. 1) are "protective" duties, charged as expedient in the national interest. Under s. 5 (1) relief therefrom may be provided in respect of the goods listed in the Third Schedule (headed "Conditional Reliefs under Treasury Order") under the restrictive conditions therein contained. Under the Finance Act 1966 further provision is made for relief from duty "in respect of goods of any description imported . . .'' into the United Kingdom, again if "expedient in the national interest". The purpose of modification (*d*) is to extend the relief provided for by s. 5 (1) and (4) of the 1958 Act, to the "protective" element contained in Revenue Duty in accordance with "relief provided for by or under the Treaties or for conformity with any Community obligation". The modification should also be considered in the light of sub-s. (6).

The test of s. 5 (1) and (4) and Sched. 3, para. 8 (as amended by the present Act, Sched. 4A (i) 1 (2) and (6)), reads:

"**5.**—(1) As respects goods of the descriptions referred to in the Third Schedule to this Act, the Secretary of State may by order provide for relieving those goods, in the circumstances, subject to the conditions and to the extent provided for by that Schedule in relation to the goods, from the whole or part of any import duty which would be chargeable on them as goods of any description.

(4) The Secretary of State may by order make provision for the administration of any relief from duty under this section *or for the implementation or administration of any like relief provided for by any Community instrument*, and may in particular—

(*a*) impose or authorise the imposition of conditions for securing that goods relieved from duty as being imported for a particular purpose are used for that purpose or such other conditions as appear expedient to secure the object or prevent abuse of the relief;

(*aa*) *where the relief is limited to a quota of imported goods, provide for determining the allocation of the quota or for enabling it to be determined by the issue of certificates or licences or otherwise*;

(*b*) confer on a government department or any other authority or person functions in connection with the administration of the relief or the enforcement of any condition of relief;

(*c*) authorise any government department having any such functions to make payments (whether for remuneration or for expenses) to persons advising the department or otherwise acting in the administration of the relief;

(*d*) require the payment of fees by persons applying for the relief or applying for the registration of any person or premises in connection with the relief;

(*e*) authorise articles for which relief is claimed to be sold or otherwise disposed of if the relief is not allowed and duty is not paid.

Sched. 3, para. 8. Goods of any description may be relieved from import duties if and in so far as the relief appears to the Treasury to be necessary or expedient with a view to conforming with an international agreement relating to matters other than commercial relations, *or with a view to conforming with any Community obligations or otherwise affording relief provided for by or under the Community Treaties*." [**33.16**]

SUB-S. (6): GENERAL NOTE

The subsection amplifies, further than sub-s. (5) (*d*) already does, the powers in respect of relief from import duties, and the further provision in that respect it enables to be made is not by virtue of s. 5 (1) and (4) of the Import Duties Act 1958 as are the powers exercisable under sub-s. (5) (*d*). It also complements sub-s. (5) (*d*) by conferring power on the Secretary of State to make regulations, providing reliefs from import duties, that do not have to be "for conformity with Community obligations"—whereas under sub-s. (5) (*d*) the powers are exercisable only for that conformity or "as regards reliefs provided for by or under the Treaties".

Regulations may be made under the subsection to amend or repeal parts of the Import Duties Act 1958, or s. 1 of the Finance Act 1966, as amended by the present Act. [**33.17**]

THE SECRETARY OF STATE MAY BY REGULATIONS . . .

The Secretary of State for Trade and Industry. See under sub-s. (1) THE SECRETARY OF STATE.

Such regulations are governed by the "Provisions as to Subordinate Legislation" set out in Sched. 2, 2 (1) and (2). They must therefore be contained in a statutory instrument, which, "if made without a draft having been approved by resolution of each House of Parliament, shall be subject to annulment in pursuance of a resolution of either House".

Regulations "as regards relief from import duties", made under the present subsection may even "amend or repeal . . . any of the provisions of Part II of the Import

Duties Act 1958 or s. 1 of the Finance Act 1966 (as modified by this Act) which are concerned with relief from import duty. As to these modifications, see Sched. 3, Part I, and Sched. 4A (i). [**33.18**]

TO BE EXPEDIENT

The only fetter on the sole discretion of the Secretary of State to decide what is or is not expedient is that he must have "regard to the practices adopted or to be adopted in other member States".

COMMUNITY OBLIGATIONS

Definition, Sched. 1, Part II, and Note.

By the definition, a Community obligation may be enforceable or not. The subsection is therefore concerned (i) with directly applicable Community law (which is made enforceable by s. 2 (1)), and (ii) with Community law which imposes any obligations *on* the United Kingdom without being directly applicable and enforceable *in* the United Kingdom. [**33.19**]

OTHER CUSTOMS SERVICES

Not necessarily only those of other member States. Co-operation by the Commissioners with the customs services of non-member States having Association Agreements with the Community is likely to be essential, for example. It may also be necessary even with the customs services of States having no agreements with the Community. But such co-operation can only be "for the purpose of implementing Community obligations"; see also GIVE EFFECT, *infra.*

(WITHOUT PREJUDICE TO THE FOREGOING) . . . FOR THAT PURPOSE

As a matter of construction, one or other of these two phrases may appear redundant. It is submitted that the proper construction is *without prejudice to co-operation with other customs services on matters of mutual concern may for the purpoe of implementing Community obligations. . . .*

(A) GIVE EFFECT

But only "for the purpose of implementing Community obligations". It follows that "any Community requirement or practice" to which effect may be given must derive from or relate to a Community obligation. (COMMUNITY OBLIGATIONS, *supra*; COMMUNITY REQUIREMENT OR PRACTICE, *infra.* Cf., also, under s. 6 (4), *post*, para. [**34.13**], SUCH PROVISION SUPPLEMENTARY. . . .)

SUCH ARRANGEMENTS AS THEY MAY DIRECT

Cf. *existing* United Kingdom law, Customs and Excise Act 1952, 47 (1): "Where any goods to which this section applies are to be shipped for exportation or as stores for use on a voyage or flight to an eventual destination outside the United Kingdom or are brought to any customs station for exportation, the exporter (*a*) shall deliver to the proper officer an entry outwards of the goods in such form and manner and containing such particulars *as the Commissioners may direct*; . . ."

OR BY REGULATIONS PRESCRIBE

The power conferred by the subsection to prescribe by regulations is not *expressed* to be a conferment "by modification or extension of an existing power" and it would appear in consequence that by virtue of Sched. 2, 2 (1) and (2) the power must be exercised by statutory instrument, which, if a draft of it has not "been approved by resolution of each House of Parliament, shall be subject to an annulment in pursuance of a resolution of either House".

Cf. under s. 6 (6) REGULATIONS.

COMMUNITY REQUIREMENT OR PRACTICE

Such must derive from or relate to a Community obligation (GIVE EFFECT, *supra*). It would appear to follow that a requirement or practice to which the subsection applies must be of general application throughout the Community and may not be one that is applied only in a single member State or in any number of member States less than the whole number, unless, which is difficult here to envisage, the Community obligation in question is imposed not by a Community Regulation or Directive, but by a Decision addressed individually to the United Kingdom and each of some other member States. And on that view, although a "practice" must be generally applied throughout the Community and relate to a Community obligation, it seems clear that it need be established only by administrative action and convenience; whereas a "requirement" must be not only of general application throughout the Community but be so because it derives from a Community obligation, and be itself enforceable as a matter of law.

See RECIPROCAL ARRANGEMENTS MADE BETWEEN MEMBER STATES, *infra*. [**33.20**]

AS TO THE MOVEMENT OF GOODS BETWEEN COUNTRIES

Such countries can only be member States, because Community law (for the implementation of obligations under which the subsection exclusively provides) cannot, by its nature, make overriding provision as to the movement of goods outside the territorial limits of the Communities. (E.E.C. Regulation 542/69, for example, applies as to transit between any two points *in* the Community. See, under Sched. 4, text of amended s. 70 of the Customs and Excise Act 1952.) [**33.21**]

(B) GIVE EFFECT

See (A) GIVE EFFECT, *supra* (and compare, under s. 6 (4), *post*, para. [**34.13**], SUCH PROVISION SUPPLEMENTARY . . .)

RECIPROCAL ARRANGEMENTS MADE BETWEEN MEMBER STATES

Such must derive from or relate to a Community obligation (GIVE EFFECT, *supra*). It would appear that arrangements to which the subsection applies must be reciprocal at least as between *all* member States (unless the Community obligation in question is imposed not by a Community Regulation or Directive, but, most unlikely, by a Decision addressed to the United Kingdom and to at least one other member State). The extension to Greece of reciprocal arrangements made between member States may serve as an example of what is intended.

Cf. COMMUNITY REQUIREMENT OR PRACTICE, *supra*. [**33.22**]

SUB-S. (8): GENERAL NOTE

The present subsection by virtue of sub-s. (9), "shall have effect as if contained in the Customs and Excise Act 1952". (For the amended text of s. 67 of the 1952 Act see under Sched. 4, *post*, para. [**62**].)

OFFICER

The Customs and Excise Act 1952, s. 307 (Interpretation), provides: " 'Officer' means, subject to the provisions of sub-s. (2) of section four of this Act, a person commissioned by the Commissioners", and s. 4 (2) provides: "any person, whether an officer or not, engaged by the orders or with the concurrence of the Commissioners (whether previously or subsequently expressed) in the performance of any act or duty relating to an assigned matter which is by law required or authorised to be performed by or with an officer, shall be deemed to be the proper officer by or with whom that act or duty is to be performed, and any person so deemed to be the proper officer shall have all the powers of an officer in relation to that act or duty." [**33.23**]

MAY REQUIRE

There is no prescribed form for such requirement. A telephone message given by an officer could suffice.

SUB-S. (9): GENERAL NOTE

The Customs and Excise Act 1952 applies to Northern Ireland (subject to the particular provisions of its s. 314 in relation to that application).

Ss. 308–312 of the 1952 Act make provision as to its applicability to the Isle of Man. All of the sections of that Act amended by s. 4 (1) and Sched. 4A (ii) 2 (1) to (7) apply to the Isle of Man so that all those amendments also apply thereto (by virtue of s. 4 (4), para. [**32.4**], *ante*). S. 258 of the 1952 Act, amended by s. 4 (1) and Sched. 4A (ii) 2 (8) does not apply to the Isle of Man.

The sections of the Customs and Excise Act 1952 as amended by s. 4 (1) and Sched. 4A (ii) 2 are set out under Sched. 4 with the amendments in italics, and with an indication of the Community secondary legislation to which they relate. [**33.24**]

6. The common agricultural policy

(1) There shall be a Board in charge of a government department, which shall be appointed by and responsible to the Ministers, and shall be by the name of the Intervention Board for Agricultural Produce a body corporate (but not subject as a statutory corporation to restrictions on its corporate capacity); and the Board (in addition to any other functions that may be entrusted to it) shall be charged, subject to the direction and control of the Ministers, with such functions

as they may from time to time determine in connection with the carrying out of the obligations of the United Kingdom under the common agricultural policy of the Economic Community.

(2) Her Majesty may by Order in Council make further provision as to the constitution and membership of the Board, and the remuneration (including pensions) of members of the Board or any committee thereof, and for regulating or facilitating the discharge of the Board's functions, including provision for the Board to arrange for its functions to be performed by other bodies on its behalf and any such provision as was made by Schedule 1 to the Ministers of the Crown Act 1964 in relation to a Minister to whom that Schedule applied; and the Ministers—

(*a*) may, after consultation with any body created by a statutory provision and concerned with agriculture or agricultural produce, by regulations modify or add to the constitution or powers of the body so as to enable it to act for the Board, or by written directions given to the body require it to discontinue or modify any activity appearing to the Ministers to be prejudicial to the proper discharge of the Board's functions; and

(*b*) may by regulations provide for the charging of fees in connection with the discharge of any functions of the Board.

(3) Sections 5 and 7 of the Agriculture Act 1957 (which make provision for the support of arrangements under section 1 of that Act for providing guaranteed prices or assured markets) shall apply in relation to any Community arrangements for or related to the regulation of the market for any agricultural produce as if references, in whatever terms, to payments made by virtue of section 1 were references to payments made by virtue of the Community arrangements by or on behalf of the Board and as if in section 5 (1) (*d*) the reference to the Minister included the Board.

(4) Agricultural levies of the Economic Community, so far as they are charged on goods exported from the United Kingdom or shipped as stores, shall be paid to and recoverable by the Board; and the powers of the Ministers to make orders under section 5 of the Agriculture Act 1957, as extended by this section, shall include power to make such provision supplementary to any directly applicable Community provision as the Ministers consider necessary for securing the payment of any agricultural levies so charged, including provision for the making of declarations or the giving of other information in respect of goods exported, shipped as stores, warehoused or otherwise dealt with.

(5) Except as otherwise provided by or under any enactment, agricultural levies of the Economic Community, so far as they are charged on goods imported into the United Kingdom, shall be levied, collected and paid, and the proceeds shall be dealt with, as if they were Community customs duties, and in relation to those levies the following enactments shall apply as they would apply in relation to Community customs duties, that is to say:—

(*a*) the general provisions of the Customs and Excise Act 1952 (as for the time being amended, whether by this or any earlier or later Act) and any other statutory provisions for the time being in force and relating to customs generally, as well as section 88 (4) of that Act as so amended; and

(*b*) sections 5, 6, 7, 10 and 13 of the Import Duties Act 1958, but so that in those sections (and in Schedule 3 to the Act), as amended by this Act, references to the Secretary of State shall include the Ministers;

and if, in connection with any such Community arrangements as aforesaid, the Commissioners of Customs and Excise are charged with the performance, on behalf of the Board or otherwise, of any duties in relation to the payment of refunds or allowances on goods exported or to be exported from the United Kingdom, then in relation to any such refund or allowance section 267 (except subsection (2) (*a*)) and section 294 of the Customs and Excise Act 1952 shall apply as they apply in relation to a drawback of customs duties, and other provisions of that Act shall have effect accordingly.

(6) The enactments applied by subsection (5) (*a*) above shall apply subject to such exceptions and modifications, if any, as the Commissioners of Customs and Excise may by regulations prescribe, and shall be taken to include section 10 of the Finance Act 1901 (which relates to changes in customs import duties in their effect on contracts), but shall not include section 259 of the Customs and Excise Act 1952 (charge of duty on manufactured or composite articles).

(7) Where it appears to the Ministers, having regard to any such Community arrangements as aforesaid (and any obligations of the United Kingdom in relation thereto), that section 1 of the Agriculture Act 1957 should cease to apply to produce of any description mentioned in Schedule 1 to that Act, they may by order made by statutory instrument, which shall be subject to annulment in pursuance of a resolution of either House of Parliament, provide that as from such date as may be prescribed by the order (but subject to such savings and transitional provisions as may be so prescribed) the Act shall have effect as if produce of that description were omitted from Schedule 1.

(8) Expressions used in this section shall be construed as if contained in Part 1 of the Agriculture Act 1957; and in this section "agricultural levy" shall include any tax not being a customs duty, but of equivalent effect, that may be chargeable in accordance with any such Community arrangements as aforesaid, and "statutory provision" includes any provision having effect by virtue of any enactment and, in subsection (2), any enactment of the Parliament of Northern Ireland or provision having effect by virtue of such an enactment. [**34**]

GENERAL NOTE

The purpose of the section is to establish a Board, named the Intervention Board for Agricultural Produce, which, subject to ministerial direction, will carry out functions connected with the implementation, so far as concerns the United Kingdom, of the common agricultural policy of the European Economic Community. The section, with a view to such implementation, provides *inter alia* for the collection and payment of agricultural levies on either exports or imports chargeable in accordance with Community arrangements, and also for commodities to be removed from the scope of the present United Kingdom agricultural guarantee system as the Community system progressively takes its place.

The section enters into force immediately upon enactment (as do the amendments of Sched. 4 to other Acts concerned with agriculture and related matters). Unlike other ss. (*e.g.*, 8 and 9) its entry into force is not deferred until on or after the "entry date", that is, 1st January 1973. This is because, before the Board can operate in practice, an Order in Council (as provided for in sub-s. (2)) is necessary to determine its constitution and membership, and the remuneration of its members. This was in fact made on 23rd October 1972, laid before Parliament 31st October 1972, to come into operation on 22nd November 1972. See S.I. No. 1578, The Intervention Board for Agricultural Produce Order 1972, [**71**], *post*. Another reason is because, in respect of contracts made at any time between enactment and 1st January 1973 for the export on or after 1st February 1973 from the United Kingdom of agricultural products, it is necessary in practice for the Board to be able to determine in advance, or give advice on, what levies will become payable on such exports. For such determination, during this interim period, a working arrangement agreed between the United Kingdom and the Economic Community will be operated. But the progressive substitution of the Community system for the United Kingdom agricultural guarantee system, referred to in the preceding paragraph, cannot commence until after the entry date. Thereafter, sub-s. (7) will enable the progressive removal of produce from the existing guarantee system to be effected, as the substitution of the new system for the existing one progresses. (The repeals effected by s. 4 (1) and Sched. 3, Parts 1 to III (but not Part IV, the repeals in which take effect on enactment) take effect on appointed dates, related to the description of the produce affected by the repeal, as substitution of one system for the other progresses.)

(Community instruments concerned with Agriculture, referred to in Art. 29 of the Act of Accession, are listed in Annex I thereto, Cmnd. 4862—II pp. 21–50, and those referred to in Art. 30 of the Act of Accession are listed in Annex II thereto, Cmnd. 4862—II, pp. 135–140). (See also Annex V, *idem* at pp. 143–146; Annex VII, *idem* at pp. 155–158; Annex XI, *idem* at pp. 165–169.) Protocol No. 16 to the Act of Accession, "on Markets and Trade in Agricultural Products" should be noted and other relevant Protocols and Declarations indexed in Cmnd. 4862—I. [**34.1**]

SUB-S. (1): GENERAL NOTE

The subsection creates, with effect from enactment, the Intervention Board for Agricultural Produce. The Board will be charged with functions, determined by the Ministers, in connection with "the carrying out of the obligations of the United Kingdom under the common agricultural policy of the Economic Community". The Board is not, in that connection, territorially restricted to the United Kingdom by the subsection.

Other functions may be entrusted to it.

THE MINISTERS

Construing this expression, as required by sub-s. (8), "as if contained in Part I of the Agriculture Act 1957", it means, by virtue of s. 11 of that Act, "the Minister of Agriculture, Fisheries and Food and the Secretaries of State respectively concerned with agriculture in Northern Ireland, acting jointly". (As to "acting jointly" see under sub-s. (2) REGULATIONS.)

By S.I. 1969 No. 388 (The Transfer of Functions (Wales) Order, 1969) Art. 3, functions relating *inter alia* to Part I of the Agriculture Act 1957 are transferred from the Minister of Agriculture, Fisheries and Food to that Minister and the Secretary of State for Wales jointly, or where so provided in Part II of Sched. 2 to the Secretary of State for Wales alone.

INTERVENTION BOARD FOR AGRICULTURAL PRODUCE ("THE BOARD")

The word "intervention" in this context is derived from Community law and practice. E.E.C. Council Regulation 729/70 of 21 April 1970 on the financing of the common agricultural policy, established as part of the Communities' budget "The European Agricultural Guidance and Guarantee Fund", and requires the "Guarantee Section" of that Fund to finance (*a*) refunds on agricultural exports to non-member countries, and (*b*) *interventions* for regulating agricultural markets. This financing is channelled through the appropriate body in each member State, and Art. 4 of the Regulation requires member States to designate the services and agencies which they empower to pay it. "The Board" will be so designated. [**34.2**]

NOT SUBJECT AS A STATUTORY CORPORATION TO RESTRICTIONS ON ITS CORPORATE CAPACITY

One effect of this provision is to render inapplicable to the Board the *ultra vires* doctrine, by which the corporate capacity of a statutory corporation is restricted, and whereby, if the subject-matter of a contract is beyond the scope of the constitution of the corporation, it is *ultra vires* and void *ab initio*, and cannot become *intra vires* by reason of ratification, estoppel, lapse of time, acquiescence, or delay. The provision is thus analogous to that of s. 9 (1) in respect of companies. (For a definition of "statutory corporation" see the Prevention of Frauds (Investments) Act 1958, s. 26 (1).) [**34.3**]

ANY OTHER FUNCTIONS

Clearly, such "other functions" are distinct from the functions referred to two lines lower down in the subsection. The latter are "in connection with the carrying out of the obligations of the United Kingdom under the common agricultural policy of the Economic Community" and are functions that "they" (the Ministers) "may from time to time determine in that connection" (see next note). "Any other functions" therefore lie outside the carrying out of common agricultural policy obligations, and are, moreover, functions with which the Ministers have no power, under the section, to charge the Board. [**34.4**]

SUCH FUNCTIONS AS THEY MAY . . . DETERMINE

Because of the power, conferred on the Ministers by the subsection, to determine the functions with which they may charge the Board in connection with the carrying out of obligations under the Community common agricultural policy, the Ministers will not be under the necessity of implementing such obligations by Statutory Instrument (since "determination of functions" is not covered by the provisions of Sched. 2, para. 2). But regulations made by the Ministers under sub-s. 2 (*a*) and (*b*) must be by statutory instrument (see sub-s. (2), *infra*) and an order made by them by virtue of sub-s. (7) must also be by statutory instrument (see sub-s. (7), *infra*).

Should regulations at any time require to be made for the purpose of implementing any Community obligation, as to which regulations the Ministers have not the necessary power under the section, the deficiency can be remedied under s. 2 (2), by an Order in Council "designating" the Minister of Agriculture, Fisheries and Food, or the department, for the purpose. [**34.5**]

SUB-S. (2): GENERAL NOTE

The subsection enables (i) further provision to be made *by Order in Council* as to the constitution and membership of the Board (and the remuneration of its members and committees) and for regulating or facilitating the discharge of its functions; and enables (ii) *the Ministers*, by regulations, to modify or add to the constitution or powers of any body created by a statutory provision and concerned with agriculture or agricultural produce, so as to enable it to act for the Board; or, by written directions to the body, to require it to discontinue or modify any activity they consider prejudicial to the proper discharge of the Board's functions; and, by regulations, to arrange for the charging of fees in connection with the discharge of any functions of the Board. [**34.6**]

ITS FUNCTIONS TO BE PERFORMED BY OTHER BODIES ON ITS BEHALF

Presumably such other bodies will be mainly statutory bodies already set up prior to enactment.

ANY SUCH PROVISION AS WAS MADE BY SCHEDULE I TO THE MINISTERS OF THE CROWN ACT 1964 . . .

For example, for the use of an official seal, as in S.I. 1972 No. 1578 "Agriculture. The Intervention Board for Agricultural Produce", paras. 7 (1), (2) and (3) "Execution and Proof of Documents", see Division III, *post*.

Schedule I to the Ministers of the Crown Act 1964, provides:—

1. The Minister shall take the oath of allegiance, and the official oath, and the Promissory Oaths Act 1868 shall have effect as if the name of the Minister were included in Part I of the Schedule to that Act.

2. The Minister may appoint such secretaries, officers and servants as he may with the consent of the Treasury determine.

3. There shall be paid to the secretaries (other than any Parliamentary Secretary), officers and servants appointed by the Minister such salaries or remuneration as the Treasury may determine.

4. The expenses of the Minister, including any salaries or remuneration payable under paragraph 3 of this Schedule, shall be defrayed out of moneys provided by Parliament.

5. The Minister shall for all purposes be a corporation sole, and shall have an official seal, which shall be authenticated by the signature of the Minister or of a secretary to the Ministry or of any person authorised by the Minister to act in that behalf.

6. The seal of the Minister shall be officially and judicially noticed, and every document purporting to be an instrument made or issued by the Minister and to be sealed with the seal of the Minister authenticated in the manner provided by paragraph 5 of this Schedule or to be signed or executed by a secretary to the Ministry or any person authorised as aforesaid, shall be received in evidence and be deemed to be so made or issued without further proof, unless the contrary is shown.

7. A certificate signed by the Minister that any instrument purporting to be made or issued by him was so made or issued shall be conclusive evidence of that fact.

8. The Documentary Evidence Act 1868 shall apply to the Minister as if his name were included in the first column of the Schedule to that Act, and as if he or a secretary to the Ministry or any person authorised by him to act on

his behalf were mentioned in the second column of that Schedule, and as if the regulations referred to in that Act included any document issued by the Minister." [**34.7**]

THE MINISTERS

See, under sub-s. (1), *supra*, THE MINISTERS

STATUTORY PROVISION

Sub-s. (8) provides: ". . . and 'statutory provision' includes any provision having effect by virtue of any enactment and, in subsection (2), any enactment of the Parliament of Northern Ireland or provision having effect by virtue of such an enactment".

REGULATIONS

Sched. 2, paras. 2 (1) and (2) apply to the power conferred on the Ministers to make regulations under (*a*) or (*b*) of the subsection; and because the power is not conferred "by modification or extension of an existing power" (Sched. 2, para. 2 (1)) it is therefore exercisable by statutory instrument, which, "if made without a draft having been approved by resolution of each House of Parliament, shall be subject to annulment in pursuance of a resolution of either House".

A statutory instrument made by "the Ministers" (THE MINISTERS, under sub-s. (1), *ante*) will not, it seems, bring into operation the provisions of Sched. 2, para. 2 (3), which are concerned with Northern Ireland. This is because the Secretary of State "concerned with agriculture in Northern Ireland", within the definition of s. 11 of the Agriculture Act 1957, "acting jointly" with the Minister of Agriculture, Fisheries and Food and the Secretary of State concerned with agriculture in Scotland, is for the time being the Secretary of State for Northern Ireland, who is a Minister of the United Kingdom Government, and not, as would be requisite for Sched. 2, para. 2 (3) to operate, "a Minister . . . of the Government of Northern Ireland." [**34.8**]

See also under s. 4 (3), LIMITATION ON THE POWERS OF THE PARLIAMENT OF NORTHERN IRELAND, *ante*, para. [**32.3**].

SUB-S. (3): GENERAL NOTE

The subsection confers powers on the Board, by providing that references in ss. 5 and 7 of the Agriculture Act 1957 to payments in support of arrangements for providing guaranteed prices or assured markets, become "references to payments made by virtue of the Community arrangements by or on behalf of the Board" (and that, so far as powers of entry upon land, and inspection, are concerned, references to the Minister include the Board).

SECTIONS 5 AND 7 OF THE AGRICULTURE ACT 1957

These provide (subject to the present subsection, whereby references in these two sections to payments in support of arrangements for providing guaranteed prices or assured markets, become "references to payments made by virtue of the Community arrangements by or on behalf of the Board" (and references in s. 5 (1) (*d*)—concerning powers of entry upon land, and inspection—to the Minister are made to include the Board)):—

5 (1) For the purpose of supporting any arrangements in force by virtue of an order under section one of this Act, and in particular of securing that payments (whether made by or on behalf of the Minister under any such order or by a Board to whom payments are so made) are made in proper cases only, the Ministers may by order make provision—

(*a*) for requiring that produce to which the order applies (being produce eligible for such payments as aforesaid or produce of any class or description which includes produce eligible for such payments) shall be marked in such circumstances, in such manner, for such purpose, and by or under the supervision of such person, as may be prescribed by or under the order;

(*b*) for prohibiting the removal from markets or other places where produce is required to be marked in pursuance of the order of any produce to which the order applies which has not been so marked;

(*c*) for requiring the producing, or the keeping and production, by merchants or other persons of books, accounts or records relating to the purchase, sale or use of produce to which the order applies;

(*d*) for enabling authorised officers of the Minister to enter upon land used for the production, storage, grading, packing, slaughter or sale of any produce to which the order applies, and to inspect and take samples of any such produce found upon land so used;

(*e*) for any other matters for which provision appears to the Minister to be necessary or expedient for the purposes described in this subsection.

(2) Without prejudice to the generality of paragraph (*e*) of subsection (1) of this section, an order under this section which applies to produce being livestock may prohibit the use for breeding or milking of any livestock marked as eligible for payments in pursuance of an order under section one of this Act.

(3) Without prejudice to the generality of the said paragraph (*e*), an order under this section which applies to produce being potatoes may prohibit—

(*a*) the sale or use for human consumption (including use in the preparation of food for human consumption);

(*b*) the sale or use for planting;

of potatoes purchased by or on behalf of the Minister or any Board in pursuance of an order under section one of this Act and sold by him or them as stockfeed.

(7) (1) If any person contravenes or fails to comply with any provision of an order under section five or section six of this Act, or knowingly has in his possession or control any livestock imported, removed or brought into the United Kingdom in contravention of an order under the said section six, he shall be liable on summary conviction to a fine not exceeding one hundred pounds or imprisonment for a term not exceeding three months or both.

(2) If any person wilfully obstructs an authorised officer or other person in the exercise of powers conferred on him by an order under section five or section six of this Act, he shall be liable on summary conviction—

(*a*) In the case of a first offence, to a fine not exceeding twenty pounds;

(*b*) in the case of a second or subsequent offence, to imprisonment for a term not exceeding one month or to a fine not exceeding fifty pounds or both.

(3) If any person—

(*a*) knowingly or recklessly makes any false statement for the purpose of obtaining for himself or any other person any sum payable in pursuance of an order under this Part of this Act;

(*b*) with intent to deceive, alters, conceals or defaces any mark applied to produce in pursuance of any such order;

(*c*) applies to produce, without due authority and with intent to deceive, any mark prescribed by or under any such order or applies to produce a mark so closely resembling a prescribed mark as to be calculated to deceive; or

(*d*) wilfully makes a false entry in any book, account of record which is required to be produced in pursuance of any such order or, with intent to deceive, makes use of any such entry which he knows to be false;

he shall be liable on summary conviction to a fine not exceeding one hundred pounds or to imprisonment for a term not exceeding three months or both, or on conviction on indictment to a fine not exceeding five hundred pounds or to imprisonment for a term not exceeding two years or both.

(4) Where an offence under this section which has been committed by a body corporate is proved to have been committed with the consent or connivance of, or to be attributable to any neglect on the part of, any director, manager, secretary or other similar officer, of the body corporate, or any person who was purporting to act in any such capacity, he as well as the body corporate shall be deemed to be guilty of that offence and shall be liable to be proceeded against and punished accordingly. [**34.9**]

SHALL APPLY

Upon enactment, but not so that the powers exercised thereunder can take effect prior to the entry date (Sched. 1, Part II, ENTRY DATE, Definition and Note).

COMMUNITY ARRANGEMENTS

The subsection makes ss. 5 and 7 of the 1957 Act (*supra*) apply in relation only to such Community arrangements as are "for or related to the regulation of the market for any agricultural produce". *For example*, the operations of the Guarantee Section of the European Agricultural Guidance and Guarantee Fund (see under sub-s. (1) INTERVEN-

TION BOARD FOR AGRICULTURAL PRODUCE) and clearly, by the terms of Art. 2 (*b*) of E.E.C. Council Regulation 729/70, arrangements for "the regulation of the market for any agricultural produce", being expressly interventions for regulating agricultural markets) and by the terms of Art. 2 (*a*) of that Regulation, are "related to" such arrangements (being "refunds on agricultural exports to non-member countries").

Such arrangements are the "arrangements as aforesaid" in sub-ss. (5), (7) and (8), *infra*. [**34.10**]

SUB-S. (4): GENERAL NOTE

The subsection is concerned with goods *exported* from the United Kingdom or shipped as stores and the agricultural levies of the Economic Community charged thereon. Imported goods are the concern of sub-s. (5).

The subsection further extends section 5 of the Agriculture Act 1957 (beyond the extension thereof already effected by sub-s. (3)) in providing that the power of the Ministers to make Orders under that section "shall include power" to make provision for securing the payment of agricultural levies of the Economic Community. This further extension is necessary because that section, even as extended by sub-s. (3), is not concerned with agricultural levies or their payment.

AGRICULTURAL LEVIES

Sub-s. (8) provides that in s. 6 "agricultural levy" shall include any tax not being a customs duty, but of equivalent effect, that may be chargeable in accordance with any such Community arrangements as aforesaid (*i.e.*, in sub-s. (3)). [**34.11**]

CHARGED ON GOODS EXPORTED FROM THE UNITED KINGDOM

Being "agricultural levies of the Economic Community", these cannot be so charged prior to 31st January 1973. This date is determined by Art. 60.1 of the Act of Accession, which provides: "In respect of products covered, on the date of accession, by a common organization of the market, the system applicable in the Communities as originally constituted in respect of customs duties and charges having equivalent effect and quantitative restrictions and measures having equivalent effect shall, subject to Articles 55 and 59, apply in the new Member States from 1st February 1973". Contracts made at any time between enactment of the section and the entry date, for the exportation *on or after the* 31*st January* 1973 of agricultural products from the United Kingdom, or their shipment as stores, require to take account of the agricultural levy of the Economic Community that will be charged on the goods so exported or shipped. Such levies "shall be paid to and recoverable by the Board", which, under a working arrangement with the Commission of the Community during the period between enactment and 1st February 1973, will be able to assess the amount of levy that any goods will attract under such contracts. [**34.12**]

SECTION 5 OF THE AGRICULTURE ACT 1957 AS EXTENDED BY THIS SECTION

This section, as extended, is set out under sub-s. (3), *supra*.

SUCH PROVISION SUPPLEMENTARY TO ANY DIRECTLY APPLICABLE COMMUNITY PROVISION AS THE MINISTERS CONSIDER NECESSARY

Cf. the new section 123A of the Food and Drugs Act 1955 inserted therein by s. 4 (1) and Sched. 4B, Food, 3 (2) (*a*).

"Such provision" must, it seems, be made by Order, as required by s. 5 of the Agriculture Act 1957 as extended by sub-s. (3).

The power of the Ministers to make such provision, is caused, by the present sub-s. (4), to be included in their power under s. 5 of the Agriculture Act 1957 as already extended by sub-s. (3). Sub-s. (4) thereby further extends s. 5 of the 1957 Act. (See the Note at the head of the present subsection.)

The use in the subsection of the expression "supplementary", rather than "complementary", could be seen as significant. A "directly applicable Community provision" can be created only in and by virtue of Community law. This is an autonomous legal order distinct from the legal order of the United Kingdom—by virtue of which latter alone, for example, Orders by United Kingdom Ministers, as in the present subsection, can acquire legal validity and force. While, therefore, provisions of the United Kingdom legal order (or of any other legal order distinct from that of the Communities) could without difficulty be regarded as made to *complement* provisions of Community law, enactment by the subsection that ministerial Orders may be made to *supplement* them seems necessarily to imply the entry at that point of the Community legal order into that of the United Kingdom. The use of the expression "supplementary" in the subsection could thus be seen as implicit recognition of the *penetration* of "directly applicable" provisions of the Community legal order *into* the legal order of the United Kingdom (cf. Introduction, *ante*, para. [**16**] *et seq.*).

There would appear in consequence to be little room for doubt that any such ministerial Order, being made "*supplementary* to any directly applicable Community provision", should be construed with reference to the directly applicable Community provision which it supplements. Clearly this must be so where the supplementary provision incorporates the directly applicable Community provision, whether textually or by reference, and is probably so even if the Community provision is not so incorporated. (Using the example of E.E.C. Council Regulation 729/70 (see under sub-s. (1) INTERVENTION BOARD FOR AGRICULTURAL PRODUCE) this is a directly applicable Community provision since Art. 189 of the E.C. Treaty provides: "A regulation shall have general application. It shall be binding in its entirety and directly applicable in all member States." Any provision supplementary to Regulation 729/70, *for example*, made by the Ministers under the subsection, that incorporated the Regulation textually or by reference, should be construed in accordance with it, and should probably be so construed even if the Regulation is not incorporated in it). [**34.13**]

SUB-S. (5): GENERAL NOTE

This subsection is concerned only with goods *imported* into the United Kingdom, and is the counterpart to sub-s. (4) which deals with exportation. Its general purpose is to equate Community agricultural levies on imports with Community customs duties, and to bring into operation (for them to be levied, collected and paid, and their proceeds dealt with in accordance with Community arrangements) the existing machinery used for the purpose of Customs and Excise together with certain provisions of the Import Duties Act 1958.

This subsection, by virtue of s. 7 (1), also takes effect, *mutatis mutandis*, "in relation to amounts charged for the use of the Sugar Board".

AGRICULTURAL LEVIES

Sub-s. (8) provides that in s. 6 "agricultural levy" shall include any tax not being a customs duty, but of equivalent effect, that may be chargeable in accordance with any such Community arrangements as aforesaid (see under sub-s. (3), *supra*, COMMUNITY ARRANGEMENTS).

CHARGED . . . LEVIED, COLLECTED AND PAID

See under s. 5 (1), *ante*, para. [**33.5**], comment under similar heading.

AS IF . . . COMMUNITY CUSTOMS DUTIES

See Sched. 1, Part II, Definition and Note; under s. 5 (1), *ante*, para. [**33.6**], SUCH COMMUNITY CUSTOMS DUTY.

SHALL APPLY

So that, by virtue of s. 5 (4), "notwithstanding that any duties are imposed for the benefit of the Communities, as if the revenue from duties so imposed remained part of the revenues of the Crown". (See, under s. 5 (4), *ante*, para. [**33.15**], AS IF THE REVENUE FROM DUTIES . . . REMAINED PART OF THE REVENUES OF THE CROWN).

(A) THE GENERAL PROVISIONS OF THE CUSTOMS AND EXCISE ACT 1952 (AS . . . AMENDED . . .)

Amendments thereto made by this Act (s. 4 (1) and Sched. 4A (ii) 2) are set out under Sched. 4, para. [**61**], *post*.

(B) REFERENCES TO THE SECRETARY OF STATE

By Sched. 4A (i) 1—(1) the Import Duties Act 1958 is amended by the substitution throughout of the words "the Secretary of State" for the words "the Board of Trade" or "the Board", and by the substitution in ss. 5, 6, 7 and 10 (but not 13) of the words "the Secretary of State" for the words "the Treasury". Cf. under s. 5 (1), THE SECRETARY OF STATE. These amendments take effect upon enactment of the present Act.

COMMUNITY ARRANGEMENTS AS AFORESAID

See under sub-s. (3), *supra*, COMMUNITY ARRANGEMENTS.

IF THE COMMISSIONERS OF CUSTOMS AND EXCISE ARE CHARGED . . . ON BEHALF OF THE BOARD . . .

See, under sub-s. (2), ARRANGE FOR ITS FUNCTIONS TO BE PERFORMED BY OTHER BODIES ON ITS BEHALF.

SECTION 267 (EXCEPT SUBSECTION (2) (*a*)) AND SECTION 294 OF THE CUSTOMS AND EXCISE ACT 1952

These provide:

267 (1) Any claim for drawback shall be made in such form and manner and contain such particulars as the Commissioners may direct.

(2) Where drawback has been claimed in the case of any goods—

(*b*) no drawback shall be paid until the person entitled thereto or his agent has made a declaration in such form and manner and containing such particulars as the Commissioners may direct that the conditions on which the drawback is payable have been fulfilled; and

(*c*) the Commissioners may require any person who has been concerned at any stage with the goods or article to furnish such information as may be reasonably necessary to enable the Commissioners to determine whether duty has been duly paid and not drawn back and for enabling a calculation to be made of the amount of drawback payable, and to produce any book of account or other document of whatever nature relating to the goods or article.

(3) If any person fails to comply with any requirement made under paragraph (*c*) of the last foregoing subsection, he shall be liable to a penalty of fifty pounds.

294 (1) Without prejudice to any other power conferred by this Act, an officer may examine and take account of any goods—

(*a*) which are imported; or
(*b*) which are in a warehouse or Queen's warehouse; or
(*c*) which have been loaded into any ship or aircraft at any place in the United Kingdom; or
(*d*) which are entered for exportation or for use as stores; or
(*e*) which are brought to any place in the United Kingdom for exportation or for shipment for exportation or as stores; or
(*f*) in the case of which any claim for drawback, allowance, rebate, remission or repayment of duty is made, and may for that purpose require any container to be opened or unpacked.

(2) Any examination of goods by an officer under this Act shall be made at such place as the Commissioners appoint for the purpose.

(3) In the case of such goods as the Commissioners may direct and subject to such conditions as they see fit to impose, an officer may permit goods to be shipped on the quay or bulked, sorted, lotted, packed or repeacked before account is taken thereof.

(4) Any opening, unpacking, weighing, measuring, repacking, bulking, sorting, lotting, marking, numbering, loading, unloading, carrying or landing of goods or their containers for the purposes of warehousing thereof shall be done and any facilities or assistance required for any such examination shall be provided by or at the expense of the proprietor of the goods.

(5) If any imported goods which an officer has power under this Act to examine are without the authority of the proper officer removed from customs charge before they have been examined those goods shall be liable to forfeiture; and any person who so removed them, if he did so with intent to defraud Her Majesty of any duty chargeable thereon or to evade any prohibition or restriction for the time being in force with respect thereto under or by virtue of any enactment, shall be liable to a penalty of three times the value of the goods or one hundred pounds, whichever is the greater, or to imprisonment for a term not exceeding two years, or to both, and may be detained.

(6) Without prejudice to the foregoing provisions of this section, where by this section or by or under any other provision of this Act an account is authorised or required to be taken of any goods for any purpose by an officer, the Commissioners may, with the consent of the proprietor of the goods, accept as the account of those goods for that purpose an account taken by such other person as may be approved in that behalf by both the Commissioners and the proprietor of the goods."

THE ENACTMENTS APPLIED BY SUBSECTION (5) (*a*)

That is, "the general provisions of the Customs and Excise Act 1952 (as for the time being amended whether by this or any earlier or later Act) and any other statutory provisions for the time being in force and relating to customs generally, as well as s. 88 (4) of that Act as so amended".

Amendments to the 1952 Act made by the present Act are set out under Sched. 4, *post*, para. [**61**] *et seq*. (S. 88 (4) as so amended is on p. 90).

SHALL APPLY

See, under sub-s. (5), *ante*, SHALL APPLY.

REGULATIONS

To be made by Statutory Instrument (Sched. 2, para. 2 (1) and (2). Cf. under s. 5 (7) OR BY REGULATIONS PRESCRIBE.

SECTION 10, FINANCE ACT 1901 AND SECTION 259, CUSTOMS AND EXCISE ACT 1952

These provide:

"**10** (1) Where any new customs import duty or new excise duty is imposed, or where any customs import duty or excise duty is increased, and any goods in respect of which the duty is payable are delivered after the day on which the new or increased duty takes effect in pursuance of a contract made before that day, the seller of the goods may, in the absence of agreement to the contrary, recover, as an addition to the contract price, a sum equal to any amount paid by him in respect of the goods on account of the new duty or the increase of duty, as the case may be.

(2) Where any customs import duty or excise duty is repealed or decreased and any goods affected by the duty are delivered after the day on which the duty ceases or the decrease in the duty takes effect in pursuance of a contract made before that day, the purchaser of the goods, in the absence of agreement to the contrary, may, if the seller of the goods has had in respect of those goods the benefit of the repeal or decrease of the duty, deduct from the contract price a sum equal to the amount of the duty or decrease of duty, as the cas may be.

(3) Where any addition to or deduction from the contract price may be made under this section on account of any new or repealed duty, such sum as may be agreed upon or in default of agreement determined by the Commissioners of Customs in the case of a customs duty, and by the Commissioners of Inland Revenue in the case of an excise duty, as representing in the case of a new duty any new expenses incurred, and in the case of a repealed duty any expenses saved, may be included in the addition to or deduction from the contract price, and may be recovered or deducted accordingly.

(4) This section shall be deemed to have had effect as from the nineteenth day of April nineteen hundred and one, and section twenty of the Customs Consolidation Act, 1876, and section eight of the Finance Act, 1900, are hereby repealed.

259 (1) Subject to the next following subsection and save where other provision is made by any other enactment relating to customs, if any imported goods contain as a part or ingredient thereof any article chargeable with a duty of customs, duty shall be chargeable on the goods in respect of each such article according to the quantity thereof appearing to the Commissioners to be used in the manufacture or preparation of the goods.

Provided that where, in the opinion of the Treasury, it is necessary for the protection of the revenue, the goods shall be chargeable with the amount of duty with which they would be chargeable if they consisted wholly of the chargeable article or, if the goods contain more than one such article, of that one of the chargeable articles which will yield the highest amount of duty.

(2) Any preparation which consists wholly or partly of extracts, essences or other concentrations of coffee or chicory shall, unless the Treasury otherwise directs, be charged with the duty chargeable on that preparation as such or with the amount of duty mentioned in the proviso to the foregoing subsection, whichever is the higher.

(3) Any rebate which can be allowed by law on any article when separately charged shall be allowed in charging goods under subsection (1) of this section in respect of any quantity of that article used in the manufacture or preparation of the goods.

SUB-S. (7): GENERAL NOTE

The subsection provides for the progressive substitution, for the guarantee system of the Agriculture Act 1957, of Community arrangements under the Common Agricultural Policy. The subsection enables the Ministers to make orders by statutory instruments so that produce of any description mentioned in Sched. 1. of the Agriculture Act 1957 may be treated as omitted from that Schedule for the purposes of the application of s. 1. of that Act to that produce and so that that Act shall have effect as if that produce were so omitted.

THE MINISTERS

See, under sub-s. (1), *supra*, THE MINISTERS.

COMMUNITY ARRANGEMENTS AS AFORESAID

See, under sub-s. (3) *supra*, COMMUNITY ARRANGEMENTS.

OBLIGATIONS OF THE UNITED KINGDOM

These are obligations "in relation" to the "Community arrangements for or related to the regulation of the market for any agricultural produce", so described in sub-s. (3), *supra*.

In requiring the Ministers, in deciding "that s. 1 of the Agriculture Act 1957 should cease to apply to produce of any description", to have regard not only to the abovementioned Community arrangements but also, by the insertion of the words in brackets to "any obligations of the United Kingdom in relation thereto", the subsection appears to place a limitative factor upon their decisions.

The obligations of the United Kingdom, in relation to the said Community arrangements, would appear to extend to those arising *indirectly*, for the purpose of securing that, in the United Kingdom, "directly applicable" Community provisions (Introduction, para. [**16**], Directly Applicable Community Law) can take their due effect. (Compare s. 2 (2) (*b*), which, in so far as it concerns "the coming into force, or the operation from time to time, of sub-s. (1)" of s. 2 appears to extend beyond the range of s. 2 (2) (*a*)). [**34.14**]

(See also Schedule 1, Part II, COMMUNITY OBLIGATION Definition and Note.)

SECTION 1, THE AGRICULTURE ACT 1957 . . . SCHEDULE 1

These state:

(1) The Minister may by order make such provision as appears to him to be expedient for providing guaranteed prices or assured markets for producers of produce described in the first Schedule to this Act.

(2) Without prejudice to the generality of the foregoing provision, an order under this section in respect of any produce may in particular provide—

(*a*) for the payment by the Minister to the Board administering a marketing scheme for the produce of sums calculated by reference to the difference between the value at guaranteed prices determined by the Minister in pursuance of the order of the produce sold by the Board and the receipts of the Board ascertained or estimated for the purposes of the order from the sale of the produce;

(*b*) for the payment by the Minister to producers of the produce, or to such other persons as may be prescribed by the order, of sums calculated by reference to the difference between guaranteed prices determined by the Minister in pursuance of the order and prices ascertained or estimated for the purpose of the order as the prices received or to be received by producers on the sale of the produce;

(*c*) for the purchase by or on behalf of the Minister or by the Board administering a marketing scheme for the produce, at guaranteed prices determined by the Minister in pursuance of the order, of any of the produce tendered by the producers, and, in the case of purchase by any such Board, for the payment by the Minister of the whole or part of any trading losses incurred or treated as incurred by the Board on the purchase and disposal of the produce.

(3) Subject to the provisions of this section, any guaranteed price to be determined by the Minister in pursuance of an order under this section shall be determined from time to time in respect of such guarantee periods (being periods of or of approximately twelve months) as may be prescribed by the order, and

shall be so determined in the light of the conclusions of the Minister from the annual review last held before the commencement of the period concerned.

(4) Subject to the following provisions of this part of this Act, any guaranteed price determined by the Minister for a guarantee period in pursuance of an order under this section may be varied by a subsequent determination of the Minister.

(5) An order under this section in respect of any produce described in the First Schedule to this Act may be made so as to apply only to particular descriptions or quantities of that produce, or may make different provision (including in particular provision for the determination of different guaranteed prices) in respect of different descriptions or quantities of that produce; and without prejudice to the generality of the foregoing provision produced may be distinguished for the purposes of any such order by reference—

(*a*) to the area in which, or the season of the year in which, it is produced, sold or despatched or delivered on sale;

(*b*) to the purpose for which it is sold or used;

(*c*) to the methods by which it is marketed, including the places at which it is delivered on sale.

(6) Where the dates of the guarantee periods prescribed by an order under this section are varied by a subsequent order, that subsequent order may direct that the duration of the first guarantee period under the order as varied, or of the last previous guarantee period, shall be shortened or extended accordingly.

FIRST SCHEDULE

Produce Qualifying for Guarantee

Part I

Crops:

Wheat
Barley
Oats
Rye
Potatoes

Part II

Livestock and Livestock Products:

Fat Cattle
Fat Sheep
Fat Pigs
Cow's Milk (Liquid)
Eggs (Hen and Duck in Shell)
Wool

PRODUCE OF ANY DESCRIPTION

As in s. 5 (1), "in relation to any goods", it is in relation to the nature of particular products that the substitution of the Community system for the United Kingdom system must be progressively brought about.

BY ORDER MADE BY STATUTORY INSTRUMENT

Cf., under sub.s (1), *supra*, SUCH FUNCTIONS AS THEY MAY DETERMINE

SUB-S. (8): GENERAL NOTE

The subsection provides for expressions used in the section to be interpreted as if contained in Part I of the Agriculture Act 1957, and defines the meanings of "agricultural levy" and "statutory provision".

PARLIAMENT OF NORTHERN IRELAND

See, under sub-s. (2) *supra*, REGULATIONS, and, under ss. 2 (5) and 4 (4), NORTHERN IRELAND. **[34.15]**

7. Sugar

(1) In relation to amounts charged for the use of the Sugar Board by a directly applicable Community provision on goods imported into the United Kingdom, and to refunds of any such amounts, section 6 (5) above shall have effect as it has effect in the case of other agricultural levies of the European Community, except that the Commissioners of Customs and Excise shall account to the Sugar Board, in such manner as the Treasury may direct, for all money collected for the benefit of the Board by virtue of that subsection and, pending payment to the Board, shall deal with all such money in such manner as the Treasury may direct.

There shall be allowed to the Commissioners, in the taking of any account under this subsection, such sums as the Treasury may from time to time determine in respect of their expenses attributable to this subsection, and the amount so allowed shall in the accounts of the Sugar Board be treated as expenses of the Board.

(2) The Minister shall, at such times as the Treasury may determine, pay to the Sugar Board any amount by which the sums charged for their benefit as mentioned in subsection (1) above, their receipts from dealings (as principals) in sugar and their other income fall short of their outgoings, whether in respect of those dealings, or of payments to be made by them in respect of imports under any directly applicable Community provision, or otherwise; but if at any time it appears to the Minister that the Sugar Board have accumulated funds in excess of the amount that they reasonably require to have available for the performance of their functions, he may direct the Board to pay to him such sum as may be specified in the direction, and the Board shall thereupon pay him the amount so specified.

(3) If as regards the home-grown beet crop for the year 1973 or any subsequent year it is made to appear to the Ministers by the processors of home-grown beet or by a body which is in their opinion substantially representative of the growers of homegrown beet that the processors and that body are unable to agree on the prices and other terms and conditions for the purchase of home-grown beet by the processors, the Ministers may determine or designate a person to determine those prices, terms and conditions; and any purchase by processors for which prices, terms and conditions have been so determined, or contract for such a purchase, shall take effect as a purchase or contract for purchase at those prices and on those terms and conditions.

(4) This section shall be construed as one with the Sugar Act 1956; and in this section, as in that Act, "the Minister" means the Minister of Agriculture, Fisheries and Food, and "the Ministers" means the Minister and the Secretary of State acting jointly. [**35**]

GENERAL NOTE

The existence of the Commonwealth Sugar Agreement (until 1974) renders it certainly more convenient to make provision as to sugar in a separate section of the Act rather than to include it within s. 6 (Agriculture) where, as an agricultural product, it logically belongs. (As to the Commonwealth Sugar Agreement, Protocol No. 17 to the Act of Accession should be noted—Cmnd. 4862—I at pp. 92–93.)

Much of the Sugar Act 1956 (with which, by virtue of sub-s. (4), the section is to be construed) is repealed by s. 4 (1) and Sched. 3, Part II, with effect from a date to be appointed. Different dates may be appointed for the repeal of different provisions to take effect (in accordance with s. 4 (2)) in a manner similar to that resulting from the operation of s. 5. (See Part II, General Note.) Some of the sections in the Sugar Act 1956 (for example, ss. 7–12 containing provisions as to surcharge on imported and home-produced sugar and molasses) need to be repealed for sheer incompatibility with Community obligations (particularly the free competition rules deriving from Arts. 85 and 86 of the E.E.C. Treaty). Repeals of some other sections serve to adapt the 1956 Act for the positive implementation of Community law as it relates to sugar.

The main purpose of the section is to provide an alternative method of financing to that comprised in the Sugar Act 1956 in its original form. (The Sugar Board, established by the 1956 Act, exercises functions under the provisions of the section which do *not* include intervention buying, but otherwise are somewhat similar to that of the Intervention Board for Agricultural Produce under s. 6). [**35.1**]

SUB-S. (1): CHARGED

Unlike Community customs duties on non-agricultural products, Community levies for the purpose of the common market in agriculture may themselves directly impose charges on the importation of sugar into a member State as "in the case of other agricultural levies of the Economic Community". The subsection does not therefore require itself to effect the imposition of the charge, but only to provide that the amounts shall be levied, collected and paid, (as also does s. 6 (5)). The subsection makes this provision by incorporating s. 6 (5). Cf. ss. 6 (5) and 5 (1) CHARGED LEVIED COLLECTED AND PAID.

SUGAR BOARD

This was established by the Sugar Act 1956 and charged with the duty, *inter alia*, "of purchasing Commonwealth sugar, at prices periodically negotiated in accordance with the Commonwealth Sugar Agreement, in fulfilment of the Government's contractual obligations under that agreement".

DIRECTLY APPLICABLE COMMUNITY PROVISION

See Sched. 1, Part II, "Community obligation", Definition and Note; Introduction, para. [**16**], *ante*. No community provision can be directly applicable to, and in, the United Kingdom prior to the entry date, 1st January 1973. (As to those that then become directly applicable, see Act of Accession, Art. 29 and Annex 1 (H) Sugar Cmnd. 4862—II, p. 18 and pp. 31–34). Such a provision may require "payments to be made by them (the Sugar Board) in respect of imports" (as referred to in sub-s. (2)) under the Community common agricultural policy.

Note the important provisions of the Act of Accession, Protocol No. 17, "On the import of sugar by the United Kingdom from the exporting countries and territories referred to in the Commonwealth Sugar Agreement." (Cmnd. 4862—I, pp. 92–93).

SECTION 6 (5) . . . SHALL HAVE EFFECT

In consequence, "amounts charged for the use of the Sugar Board . . ." covered by the present subsection, "shall be levied, collected and paid, and the proceeds shall be dealt with, as if they were Community customs duties . . ."

Like the present subsection, s. 6 (5) is concerned only with *imported* goods.

OTHER AGRICULTURAL LEVIES

The levy on sugar is itself an agricultural levy. By virtue of s. 6 (8), the expression "agricultural levies" (in s. 6 (5) which here applies) "shall include any tax not being a customs duty, but of equivalent effect, that may be chargeable in accordance with any such arrangements as aforesaid" (*viz.* in s. 6 (3)).

OF THE EUROPEAN COMMUNITY

This must mean of the *Economic* Community, as in s. 6 (5). (There is no such thing as *the* European Community; there are the European Communit*ies*.) [**35.2**]

FOR THE BENEFIT OF THE BOARD

All money collected, under this head, by the Commissioners of Customs and Excise, and paid to the Board, is added to the Board's receipts from dealings (as principals) in sugar, and to their other income. If the total falls short of the Board's outgoings (as defined in sub-s. (2)) "the Minister shall, at such times as the Treasury may determine, pay to the Sugar Board" the amount of the shortfall (sub-s. (2)).

SUB-S. (2): THE MINISTER

The Minister of Agriculture, Fisheries and Food (sub-s. (4)).

SUGAR BOARD

See under sub-s. (1), *supra*, SUGAR BOARD.

(AS PRINCIPALS)

The Sugar Act 1956 s. 1 (2) (*b*); and s. 1 (5): "For the purposes of this Act all sugar purchased by the Sugar Board shall be taken to be purchased by them as principals, except in the case of sugar which they are expressly directed to purchase as agents of the Minister"; and s. 1 (6): "The price at which the Sugar Board shall sell sugar, which they have purchased as principals, shall be such as appears to the Board to be the best price reasonably obtainable for the sugar, having regard to the date of delivery and other terms and conditions of the sale".

OTHER INCOME

For example, from investment in the British Sugar Corporation Limited.

DIRECTLY APPLICABLE COMMUNITY PROVISION

See, under sub-s. (1), DIRECTLY APPLICABLE COMMUNITY PROVISION.

SUB-S. (3): GENERAL COMMENT
The purpose of the subsection is to replace, as far as necessary for the purpose of the Act, the provisions of the Sugar Act 1956, s. 17, repealed with effect from the appointed date by s. 4 (1) and Sched. 3, Part II.

THE MINISTERS
"The Minister and the Secretary of State acting jointly", sub-s. (4), *infra*.

BY A BODY . . .
Such as the National Farmers Union.

MAY DETERMINE OR DESIGNATE A PERSON TO DETERMINE
The power of the Ministers conferred by this provision is in respect of the *prices*, *terms* and *conditions* for the purchase of home-grown beet by the processors. The provision replaces, with effect from the appointed date, the Sugar Act 1956, s. 17 (2): "The prices to be paid by the (British Sugar) Corporation under contracts for the purchase of home-grown beet shall be such *prices* as may be determined by or under any directions of the Ministers given in that behalf . . .", and s. 17 (3): "In other respects the *terms* and *conditions* contained in such contracts shall be such terms and conditions as may, with the approval of the Ministers, be agreed between the (British Sugar) Corporation and any body which, in the opinion of the Ministers, is substantially representative of the growers of home-grown beet, or in default of any such agreement, shall be such as may be determined by the Ministers." [**35.3**]

CONSTRUED AS ONE WITH
S. 4 (3) does not apply because the Sugar Act 1956 itself extends to Northern Ireland (see next comment) and there are no "provisions having effect only in Northern Ireland" to which the 1956 Act is "similar in purpose".

THE SUGAR ACT 1956
Extends to Northern Ireland with the exception of ss. 17–24 (s. 36 (3) of the 1956 Act). Ss. 7–16 and 33–35 (so far as they have effect for the purposes of ss. 7–16) extend to the Isle of Man (s. 36 (2) of the 1956 Act). [**35.4**]

8. Cinematograph films

(1) On and after the entry date Community films shall be registered under the Films Acts 1960 to 1970 as a class distinct from other foreign films, and be registered as quota films, and the register shall be kept accordingly; and —

(*a*) references in those Acts to a foreign film, except in sections 11 and 17 of the Films Act 1960 (which relate to registration) shall have effect as references to a foreign film other than a Community film; and

(*b*) references to a British film shall in the following provisions of the Films Act 1960 have effect as references to a British or Community film, that is to say, in sections 1 (1), 2 (2) (as set out in section 10 (1) of the Films Act 1970), 30 (3) (*b*), 32 (1) (*b*) and 44 (1) (*b*).

In this subsection and in subsection (2) below "Community film" means any such film as in accordance with any relevant Community instrument is to be regarded as a film of a member State.

(2) Where a film which on the entry date is registered under the Films Act 1960 as a foreign film is a Community film, a person who has the right to distribute the film or is in a position to confer that right may apply for the register to be amended by registering the film as a Community film; and if the application is accompanied by the requisite particulars and evidence to show the film is a Community film, and by such fee as may be prescribed for this purpose under section 44 of the Act, the register shall be amended accordingly and there shall be issued to the applicant, in substitution for any certificate of registration previously issued, a certificate of registration specifying the particulars of the film as recorded in the register after the amendment.

In relation to a film registered as a Community film by virtue of this subsection, section 2 of the Films Act 1960 (disregard of old films for quota purposes) shall have effect as if in subsection (2), whether as originally enacted or as set out in section 10 (1) of the Films Act 1970, the reference to a film being first registered as a British film were a reference to its being first registered.

(3) The requirements for the registration of a film as a British film under section 17 of the Films Act 1960 shall be modified, with effect from the entry date, by inserting after the words "of the Republic of Ireland", wherever those words occur in section 17 (2) (*a*) and (3), the words "or of any country that is a member State".

(4) If, on the application of an exhibitor in respect of a cinema, the Secretary of State is satisfied that during the year 1973 or any later year it is proposed to exhibit at the cinema no films other than foreign language films, he may (after consultation with the Cinematograph Films Council) direct that section 1 of the Films Act 1960 shall not apply to the exhibition of films at that cinema during that year; but section 1 shall nevertheless apply as if no such direction had been given—

(*a*) where during the year any film other than a foreign language film is exhibited at the cinema; and

(*b*) where, on the application of an exhibitor who exhibits films at the cinema, the Secretary of State substitutes for the direction a direction under section 4 (1) of the Act.

In this subsection "foreign language film" means a film in which the dialogue is mainly in a foreign language.

(5) This section shall be construed as one with the Films Act 1960. [**36**]

GENERAL NOTE

The main purpose of the section is twofold: to enable Community films to be reckoned in the quota of films required, by s. 1 of the Films Act 1960, to be shown by exhibitors in Great Britain; and to remove discrimination on grounds of possessing the nationality of any member State of the Communities, against individuals and companies, thus enabling them to make what, for purposes of the Films Act 1960, is a "British film".

The Films Act 1960 (with which sub-s. (5) requires the section to be construed) "except so much thereof as relates to the powers of the Parliament of Northern Ireland and to the Copyright Act 1956", does not extend to Northern Ireland (Films Act 1960, s. 52 (4)). Since there are no provisions as to cinematograph films "having effect only in Northern Ireland" to which the Films Act 1960 could be considered "similar in purpose", there is consequently no need for legislative action by virtue of s. 4 (3) to ensure that Community law on this subject can take effect there.

Though not expressed so to do, the section implements the Community obligations of the United Kingdom created by the following E.E.C. Council Directives: 63/607, based in particular on Art. 63 (2) of the E.E.C. Treaty and "implementing in respect of the film industry the provisions of the General Programme for the abolition of restrictions on freedom to provide services"; 65/264 based in particular on Arts. 54 (2) and (3) and 63 (2) of the E.E.C. Treaty and "implementing in respect of the film industry the provisions of the General Programmes for the abolition of restrictions on freedom of establishment and freedom to provide services"; 68/369 based in particular on Art. 54 (2) and (3) of the E.E.C. Treaty and "concerning the attainment of freedom of establishment in respect of activities of self-employed persons in film distribution". Directive 70/451, based on the same Treaty Articles (as well as on Art. 63 (2) and (3)) and concerning "the attainment of freedom of establishment and freedom to provide services in respect of activities of self-employed persons in film production" is amended by the Act of Accession (Cmnd. 4862—11, pp. 65–66) which adds a new sub-para. (3) to para. 2 of Art. 3 of that Directive requiring the abolition of "the rule that only a company registered in, and the central management and control of whose business is exercised in, the United Kingdom shall be eligible for a payment from the British Film Fund (s. 3 (1) (ii) of S.I. 1970 No. 1146)": the Directive, as so amended will require that the definition of what is an "eligible film" for purposes of the Cinematograph Films Act 1957 and of the section of S.I. 1970 No. 1146 referred to, be amended accordingly.

(See, for the list of Community instruments concerning the Cinema provided for in Art. 29 of the Act of Accession, Annex I thereto—Cmnd. 4862—II, pp. 65–6). **[36.1]**

SUB-S. (1): ENTRY DATE

Sched. 1, Part II, Definition and Note.

OTHER FOREIGN FILMS

Other could be regarded as surplusage. The purpose of the subsection is to equate Community films to British films (for purposes of the quota only). From the entry date what pertains to the Communities ceases to be "foreign" (in the traditional sense) for the United Kingdom. Community law, *for example*, is thenceforth not foreign law in the United Kingdom and does not, like foreign law, require to be proved as fact before a United Kingdom court, which, under s. 3 (2), is required to take judicial notice of it. A "Community film", as defined in the last sentence of the subsection is only foreign in the sense that it "is to be regarded as a film of a member State". Cf. the wording in sub-s. (2): "Where a film . . . registered . . . as a foreign film is a Community film . . . apply for the register to be amended . . ." **[36.2]**

IN ACCORDANCE WITH ANY RELEVANT COMMUNITY INSTRUMENT . . . FILM OF A MEMBER STATE

As to "Community instrument" see Sched. 1, Part II, Definition and Note. The principal "relevant Community instrument", for the purposes of the subsection, is E.E.C. Council Directive 63/607, (*Official Journal* No. 159 of 2.11.63, p. 2661/63), which defines the term "film" and lays down common criteria for recognition of the nationality of films of member States (see General Note, *supra*).

On 3rd April 1964 the European Commission issued a Recommendation addressed to the member States concerning the nationality of films provided for in Article 11 of the above-mentioned directive. Thereby, the film which is to be certified as the national film of a member State in accordance with Directive 63/607 shall be certified as such by means of a certificate of nationality in the form attached to the recommendation. Member States will normally accept such certificates as sufficient evidence of the film's nationality in accordance with the definition in Directive 63/607.

SUB-S. (2): ENTRY DATE

Sched. 1, Part II, Definition and Note.

REQUISITE PARTICULARS AND EVIDENCE

See, under sub-s. (1), IN ACCORDANCE WITH ANY RELEVANT COMMUNITY INSTRUMENT

Cf. the wording in the Films Act, 1960, s. 44 (1) (*b*): "the particulars and evidence necessary for satisfying the Board that a film ought to be registered as a British film or as a quota film".

SECTION 2 OF THE FILMS ACT 1960

S. 2 (2) of the Films Act 1960 (as originally enacted in 1960 and not as amended by s. 10 (1) of the Films Act 1970) continues to apply to films registered before 1st January 1971. The provision concerns the quota life of films registered before that date; it will cease to have effect at the end of 1975 at the latest, when the quota life of any such film will expire.

SUB-S. (3): ENTRY DATE

Schedule 1, Part II, Definition and Note.

INSERTING . . . THE WORDS "OR OF ANY COUNTRY THAT IS A MEMBER STATE"

The insertion of these words in s. 17 (2) (*a*) and (3) of the Films Act 1960 removes discrimination, on grounds of possessing the nationality of any member State of the Communities, against individuals and companies, thus enabling them to make, for the purposes of that Act, a "British film". As a result of the insertion a film may, after the entry date, be registered as a British film if "the maker of the film was, throughout the time during which the film was being made", either a British subject, or a citizen of the Republic of Ireland, or a citizen of any member State of the Communities, or, if a company, (*a*) was incorporated under the laws of any Commonwealth country, or of the Republic of Ireland, or of any country that is a member State of the Communities, *and* (*b*) its directors, or the majority of its directors, are British subjects or citizens of the Republic of Ireland, or of any country that is a member State of the Communities.

It should be noted that, in s. 17 of the Films Act 1960,

" 'Maker', in relation to a film, means the person by whom the arrangements necessary for the making of the film are undertaken." (S. 50 (1), Films Act, 1960). So far as the definition in the 1960 Act concerns newsreels, s. 1 (3) of the Films Act 1964 substitutes "editing" for "making" in that definition. The "maker" of a film is not the "film director", but is commonly referred to alternatively as the "producer" (though he is not a producer in the sense in which that word is used in the expression "theatrical producer"). [**36.3**]

SUB-S. (4): GENERAL NOTE

The position under the Films Act 1960 has been, prior to the enactment of this subsection, that no cinema exhibiting exclusively foreign language films could lawfully exist. Section 1 (1) of that Act provides: "British films shall be included, . . . among the registered films exhibited by an exhibitor while the section is in force."

CINEMATOGRAPH FILMS COUNCIL

The Council was established by s. 41 of the Films Act 1960 and its constitution is set out in the First Schedule to that Act.

The requirement imposed by the present subsection on the Secretary of State to consult the Council relates to s. 4 (1) of the Films Act 1960 (as amended by s. 12 (1) of the Films Act 1970) whereby the Secretary of State may prescribe a reduced percentage (quota) in respect of cinemas which fall into certain prescribed categories. The present Act adds a further category and provides for the same requirement.

THE DIALOGUE IS MAINLY IN A FOREIGN LANGUAGE

Welsh is not a "foreign language" (note the Welsh Language Act 1967 (*c.* 66)) nor are some other languages.

SUB-S. (5): GENERAL NOTE

S. 22 (1) (*c*) of the Films Act, 1970, provides: "this Act and the Films Acts 1960 to 1966 may be cited together as the Films Acts 1960 to 1970". By implication, the reference in sub-s. (5) appears to be to the Films Act 1960, as amended by the Films Act 1966 and 1970.

CONSTRUED AS ONE WITH

S. 4 (3) does *not* in consequence need to be applied, because although the Films Act 1960 "except so much thereof as relates to the powers of the Parliament of Northern Ireland and to the Copyright Act, 1956, does not extend to Northern Ireland" (Films Act 1960, s. 52 (4)) there are no similar provisions "having effect only in Northern Ireland". There are no legislative restrictions in Northern Ireland relating to cinematograph films needing to be repealed or amended in order to permit the due application of Community law. [**36.4**]

9. Companies

(1) In favour of a person dealing with a company in good faith, any transaction decided on by the directors shall be deemed to be one which it is within the capacity of the company to enter into, and the power of the directors to bind the company shall be deemed to be free of any limitation under the memorandum or articles of association; and a party to a transaction so decided on shall not be bound to enquire as to the capacity of the company to enter into it or as to any such limitation on the powers of the directors, and shall be presumed to have acted in good faith unless the contrary is proved.

(2) Where a contract purports to be made by a company, or by a person as agent for a company, at a time when the company has not been formed, then subject to any agreement to the contrary the contract shall have effect as a contract entered into by the person purporting to act for the company or as agent for it, and he shall be personally liable on the contract accordingly.

(3) The registrar of companies shall cause to be published in the Gazette notice of the issue or receipt by him of documents of any of the following descriptions (stating in the notice the name of the company, the description of document and the date of issue or receipt), that is to say—

(*a*) any certificate of incorporation of a company;
(*b*) any document making or evidencing an alteration in the memorandum or articles of association of a company;
(*c*) any return relating to a company's register of directors, or notification of a change among its directors;
(*d*) a company's annual return;
(*e*) any notice of the situation of a company's registered office, or of any change therein;
(*f*) any copy of a winding-up order in respect of a company;
(*g*) any order for the dissolution of a company on a winding up;
(*h*) any return by a liquidator of the final meeting of a company on a winding up;

and in the following provisions of this section "official notification" means, in relation to anything stated in a document of any of the above descriptions, the notification of that document in the Gazette under this section and, in relation to the appointment of a liquidator in a voluntary winding up, the notification thereof in the Gazette under section 305 of the Companies Act 1948, and "officially notified" shall be construed accordingly.

(4) A company shall not be entitled to rely against other persons on the happening of any of the following events, that is to say—

(*a*) the making of a winding-up order in respect of the company, or the appointment of a liquidator in a voluntary winding up of the company; or
(*b*) any alteration of the company's memorandum or articles of association; or
(*c*) any change among the company's directors; or
(*d*) (as regards service of any document on the company) any change in the situation of the company's registered office;

if the event had not been officially notified at the material time and is not shown by the company to have been known at that time to the person concerned, or if the material time fell on or before the fifteenth day after the date of official notification (or, where the fifteenth day was a non-business day, on or before the next day that was not) and it is shown that the person concerned was unavoidably prevented from knowing of the event at that time.

For this purpose "non-business day" means a Saturday or Sunday, Christmas Day, Good Friday and any other day which, in the part of Great Britain where the company is registered, is a bank holiday under the Banking and Financial Dealings Act 1971.

(5) Where any alteration is made in a company's memorandum or articles of association by any statutory provision, whether contained in an Act of Parliament or in an instrument made under an Act, a printed copy of the Act or instrument shall not later than fifteen days after that provision comes into force be forwarded to the registrar of companies and recorded by him; and where a company is required by this section or otherwise to send to the registrar any document making or evidencing an alteration in the company's memorandum or articles of association (other than a special resolution under section 5 of the Companies Act 1948), the company shall send with it a printed copy of the memorandum or articles as altered.

If a company fails to comply with this subsection, the company and any officer of the company who is in default shall be liable to a default fine.

(6) Where before the coming into force of this subsection—

(*a*) an alteration has been made in a company's memorandum or articles of association by any statutory provision, and a printed copy of the relevant Act or instrument has not been sent to the registrar of companies; or

(*b*) an alteration has been made in a company's memorandum or articles of association in any manner, and a printed copy of the memorandum or articles as altered has not been sent to him;

such a copy shall be sent to him within one month after the coming into force of this subsection.

If a company fails to comply with this subsection, the company and any officer of the company who is in default shall be liable to a default fine.

(7) Every company shall have the following particulars mentioned in legible characters in all business letters and order forms of the company, that is to say,—

(*a*) the place of registration of the company, and the number with which it is registered;

(*b*) the address of its registered office; and

(*c*) in the case of a limited company exempt from the obligation to use the word "limited" as part of its name, the fact that it is a limited company;

and, if in the case of a company having a share capital there is on the stationery used for any such letters or on the order forms a reference to the amount of the share capital, the reference shall be to paid-up share capital.

If a company fails to comply with this subsection, the company shall be liable to a fine not exceeding £50; and if an officer of a company or any person on its behalf issues or authorises the issue of any business letter or order form not complying with this subsection, he shall be liable to a fine not exceeding £50.

(8) This section shall be construed as one with the Companies Act 1948; and section 435 of that Act (which enables certain provisions of it to be extended to unregistered companies) shall have effect as if this section were among those mentioned in Schedule 14 to that Act with an entry in column 3 of that Schedule to the effect that this section is to apply so far only as may be specified by regulations under section 435 and to such bodies corporate as may be so specified, and as if sections 107 (registered office) and 437 (service of documents) were so mentioned (and section 437 were not included in the last entry in the Schedule).

The modifications of this section that may be made by regulations under section 435 shall include the extension of subsections (3), (5) and (6) to additional matters (and in particular to the instruments constituting or regulating a company as well as to alterations thereof).

(9) This section shall not come into force until the entry date (except to authorise the making with effect from that date of regulations by virtue of subsection (8) above). [**37**]

GENERAL NOTE

This Section effects a number of amendments of United Kingdom law governing companies, in order to bring it into conformity with Community law. In fact, *though not expressed so to do*, the section adapts United Kingdom company law to the requirements of Community law that were already in force at the date of signature of the Treaty of

Accession (22nd January 1972), namely, the E.E.C. Council Directive on corporations, 68/151, amended as provided by the Act of Accession (Art. 29) in Annex I thereto (Cmnd. 4862—II, at p. 67). (That Directive was "designed to co-ordinate and thus bring the guarantees required of corporate bodies in member States within the terms of Art. 58, paragraph 2, of the E.E.C. Treaty, to protect the interests of members and third parties". Its concern is with the Right of Establishment in Community law, with particular regard to Art. 54, paragraph 3 (*g*) of that Treaty.)

But no Community obligation falls on the United Kingdom to comply with that Directive prior to the entry date (1st January 1973) and it is accordingly provided by sub-s. (9) that the section shall not come into force until that date (except to authorise the making, following its enactment, and by virtue of sub-s. (8), of regulations under s. 435 of the Companies Act 1948 to take effect from the entry date).

The section is to be construed as one with the Companies Act 1948 (sub-s. (8)). It is submitted that, in general, it must be construed in accordance with the accepted rules for the interpretation of statutes and that (although regard will consequently be had to the fact that the section is contained in the part of the Act entitled "Amendment of Law" and the Act itself is expressed "to make provision in connection with the enlargement of the European Communities to include the United Kingdom . . ." see comment under THE LONG TITLE, para. [**28.1**], *ante*) recourse should not normally be made for purposes of construction to the wording of the Community directive that in fact, though not expressly, the section implements. [**37.1**]

SUB-S. (1): GENERAL NOTE

The subsection modifies the *ultra vires* doctrine. (Cf. the modification of that doctrine in its application to a statutory corporation, with regard to the Intervention Board for Agricultural Produce established by s. 6 (1)).

IN GOOD FAITH

This expression is not defined in the Act and is not used in the Companies Act (1948), with which Act the section is required by sub-s. 8 to be construed as one; it is not commonly used in company law practice, in which "not acting fraudulently" appears to be the nearest equivalent. (It may also be noted, though the point can here be no more than indirectly relevant, that though "in good faith" is frequently used in the laws of the Community countries, it does not appear in E.E.C. Council Directive 68/151, which is, in fact, though not expressed so to be, implemented by the section. It seems doubtful whether the expression "a purchaser in good faith" defined in and for the purpose of s. 157 (2) of the Law of Property Act 1925, or as used in s. 3 (3) of the Land Charges Act 1925 (Pending Actions) can be called in aid in construing "in good faith" in the present subsection). [**37.2**]

THE DIRECTORS

The expression includes "a director" by virtue of s. 1 of the Interpretation Act 1889. S. 455 of the Companies Act 1948, its interpretation section, defines "director" only in the singular, as including "any person occupying the position of director by whatever name called".

FREE OF ANY LIMITATION UNDER THE MEMORANDUM OR ARTICLES

Consequently, *not* free of any limitation contained, for example, in a managing director's service agreement with the company; the words "any such limitation" two lines from the end of the subsection mean "any limitation under the memorandum or articles".

PRESUMED . . . UNLESS THE CONTRARY IS PROVED

By this provision, the burden of proof is shifted to the company where it formerly rested on a person contracting with the company.

SUB-S. (2): GENERAL NOTE

The subsection makes provision in respect of pre-incorporation contracts.

CONTRACT SHALL HAVE EFFECT

Since the contract "shall have effect as a contract entered into by the person purporting to act for the company or as agent for it" it follows that that person may in his personal capacity both sue and be sued on the contract, and the necessity for the remaining words of the subsection is not altogether apparent.

The effect is to remove the necessity for the distinction, formerly made, between a person purporting to act for a company before its incorporation, who signs a contract as *agent* for that company and a person so purporting who signs as a *director* of it:

Kelner v. *Baxter* (1866), L.R.2 C.P.174 and *Newborne* v. *Sensolid* (*Great Britain*), *Ltd.*, [1953] 1 Q.B. 45. **[37.3]**

SUB-S. (3): GENERAL NOTE

The subsection provides for publication in the Gazette of notice of a wide range of company documents in respect of which such publicity was not formerly required.

Notice of none of the documents in any of the categories (*a*) to (*h*) inclusive, was, prior to the Act, required for any purpose to be published in the Gazette. To describe such notice, the subsection introduces the technical expression "official notification", defines that expression, and provides that notification under s. 305 of the Companies Act 1948, of the appointment of a liquidator in a voluntary winding up, shall be construed as "official notification". The effect, as against other persons, of the absence of official notification at the material time of any document in categories (*b*), (*c*)—as to a change among a company's directors, (*e*)—as to any change in the situation of the company's registered office (and as regards service of any document on the company) and (*f*), as well as of the absence of official notification under s. 305 of the appointment of a liquidator in a voluntary winding up of the company, is, as provided by sub-s. (4) and subject to the exceptions therein contained, that the company "shall not be entitled to rely . . . on the happening of . . ." the event officially notifiable in the manner provided by sub-s. (3).

With regard to (*b*) (alteration in the memorandum or articles) it should be noted that sub-s. (5) makes provision with regard to any such alteration by Act of Parliament or statutory instrument and that sub-s. (6) makes provision for any such alteration made by Act of Parliament or statutory instrument before the coming into force of that subsection. **[37.4]**

SUB-S. (4): GENERAL NOTE

All the events listed in (*a*) to (*d*) inclusive may be "officially notified" in the sense of sub-s. (3) and as therein provided. With the exception of the appointment of a liquidator in a voluntary winding-up (listed as the second alternative event covered by (*a*), which is notifiable under s. 305 of the Companies Act 1948) all the events in (*a*) to (*d*) are provided for in sub-s. (3) as follows:

(*a*) (first alternative event by sub-s. (3) (*f*)
(*b*) by sub-s. (3) (*b*)
(*c*) by sub-s. (3) (*c*)
(*d*) by sub-s. (3) (*e*)

SUB-S. (5): GENERAL NOTE

This subsection makes provision in relation to the registration of any alteration in a company's memorandum or articles made *on or after the entry date* by a statutory provision. The following sub-s. (6) provides correspondingly in regard to such an alteration made *before* the entry date.

The requirements of sub-s. (3) (*b*) should be noted.

SHALL BE FORWARDED TO THE REGISTRAR OF COMPANIES

These words impliedly impose a duty *on the Company*, because of the words that follow later: "If a company fails to comply . . . default fine".

BY THIS SECTION OR OTHERWISE

As to "or otherwise", the following sections of The Companies Act 1948 pertain:

> S. 69 requires delivery to the registrar for registration of a copy of the order of Court confirming the reduction of the share capital of a company and of a minute, approved by the Court, showing the amount of the share capital as so reduced, the number of shares, of what amount each, into which it is divided, and the amount deemed to be paid up on each share at the date of registration. The reduction of share capital cannot take effect before registration in the above way.
>
> S. 72 (5) requires the company to forward to the registrar a copy of the order of the Court made on an application under the section in respect of the variation of shareholders' rights.
>
> S. 143 requires a printed copy to be forwarded to the Registrar of any special resolution; extraordinary resolution; a resolution agreed to by all the members of a company which would not otherwise have been effective for its purpose unless it had been passed, as the case may be, as a special or as an extraordinary resolution; a resolution or agreement agreed to by all the members of some class of shareholders which otherwise would have been ineffective for its

purpose unless passed by some particular majority or in some other particular manner, and any resolution which effectively binds all the members of any class of shareholders though not agreed to by all those members; and any resolution requiring a company to be wound up voluntarily, passed under paragraph (*a*) of sub-s. (1) of s. 278 of the Act.

S. 206 (3) requires an office copy of an order of the Court sanctioning a compromise or arrangement to be delivered to the registrar for registration. The compromise or arrangement cannot take effect before such registration.

S. 210 (4) requires an office copy of an order of the Court, made on a petition by a member that the affairs of a company are being conducted in a manner oppressive to some part of the members (including himself) or in a petition by the Board of Trade in a case falling within s. 169, to be delivered to the registrar for registration.

OFFICER OF THE COMPANY

The Companies Act 1948, s. 455: provides "'Officer', in relation to a body corporate, includes a director, manager or secretary".

DEFAULT FINE

Companies Act 1948, s. 440. Applying s. 440 (1), "default fine" in the present subsection ("construed as one with the Companies Act 1948" (sub-s. (8)) means "for every day during which the default continues . . . a fine not exceeding five pounds". But, applying s. 440 (2) "any officer . . . who is in default" means any officer of the company, as defined in s. 455, "who knowingly and wilfully authorizes or permits the default, refusal or contravention mentioned in the enactment".

SUB-S. (6): GENERAL NOTE

The subsection makes provision in relation to the registration of any alteration in a company's memorandum or articles made, *before the entry date*, by a statutory provision or in any manner. It requires a printed copy of the relevant Act, or instrument, or a printed copy of the memorandum or articles as altered otherwise than by a statutory provision, to be sent to the Registrar within one month of the entry date (1st January 1973).

Such alterations, made by statutory provision, *on and after the entry date*, are provided for by the preceding sub-s. (5). **[37.5]**

BY ANY STATUTORY PROVISION

Clearly, as in sub-s. (5), this means "whether contained in an Act of Parliament or in an instrument made under an Act", since in the words that follow in (*a*) there is reference to a "printed copy of the relevant Act or instrument . . ."

SHALL BE SENT

See under sub-s. (5), SHALL BE FORWARDED TO THE REGISTRAR OF COMPANIES.

The words in sub-s. (6) carry the same implication.

OFFICER

See, under sub-s. (5), OFFICER OF THE COMPANY.

DEFAULT FINE

See, under sub-s. (5), DEFAULT FINE.

SUB-S. (7): GENERAL NOTE

This subsection sets out the particulars that it requires to be mentioned in a company's business letters and order forms.

"(*a*) . . . THE NUMBER WITH WHICH IT IS REGISTERED", is the registration number which appears on a company's certificate of incorporation.

(*c*) refers to charities and certain other companies, permitted, under s. 19 of the Companies Act 1948, to be "registered as a company with limited liability, without the addition of the word 'limited' to its name . . .'

The inclusion of a reference to the amount of a company's share capital on the stationery used for its business letters or on its order forms is not obligatory. The main reason why, where there is such a reference, it must be to paid-up share capital, appears to be that the concepts of nominal and issued capital are relatively little used in the company law of the other member States of the European Communities. **[37.6]**

PAID-UP SHARE CAPITAL

"Paid-up capital" in the subsection presumably includes capital credited as fully-paid. Construing the subsection as one with the Companies Act 1948, as required by sub-s. (8), does not produce a contrary result. As regards the matters to be specified in a company Prospectus, it is required by s. 38 of that Act and para. 8 of its Fourth Schedule that "the number and amount of shares and debentures which within the two preceding years have been issued, or agreed to be issued, as fully or partly paid up otherwise than in cash"... be specified. As regards a Company's Annual Return, s. 124 together with Part I, para. 3 of the Sixth Schedule of the Companies Act 1948, requires "a summary, distinguishing between shares issued for cash and shares issued as fully or partly paid up on the shares", thus retaining the distinction. But the phrase "paid-up" or "fully paid-up" shares does not figure in the list of expressions defined in s. 455 of the Act; the Eighth Schedule, containing "General Provisions as to Balance Sheet and Profit and Loss Account" requires a summary *inter alia* of the authorized and issued share capital but does not use the expression "paid-up"; s. 52, in respect of registration of a return of allotment of shares, makes in sub-s. (1) (*b*) special provision "in the case of shares allotted as fully or partly paid up otherwise than in cash"; though *Buckley on the Companies Act*, 13th edition, 1957, p. 142, points out that "where shares are paid-up in kind . . ." they "must be treated as fully paid-up" as a normal rule, the four exceptions to which are those listed; and, in respect of alteration of a company's share capital s. 61 (1) (*c*) referring to "paid-up shares" makes no distinction between shares paid-up and those credited as paid-up. [**36.7**]

SUB-S. (8): GENERAL NOTE

The effect of the subsection is that service of documents on an unregistered company must now be made in accordance with the Rules of the Supreme Court. It is, on and after the entry date, no longer lawful to effect such service under s. 437 of the Companies Act 1948, by virtue of s. 435 and subject to the limitations therein provided for. [**37.8**]

CONSTRUED AS ONE WITH THE COMPANIES ACT 1948

In consequence, the provisions of s. 4 (3) become applicable, for the following reasons. S. 9 is "one of the following sections of the Act" which "is construed as one with an Act . . . similar in purpose to provisions having effect only in Northern Ireland . . ." (s. 4 (3)); the Companies Act 1948 does not apply to companies registered or incorporated in Northern Ireland (except as oversea companies in Great Britain) and nothing contained therein "shall affect the law in force in Northern Ireland at the commencement of this Act" (s. 461); the Companies Act 1948 is "similar in purpose to" the Companies Act (Northern Ireland). [**37.9**]

MODIFICATIONS OF THIS SECTION . . . BY REGULATIONS UNDER S. 435

Any regulations under s. 435 must be made by statutory instrument (s. 435 (5)).

SUB-S. (9): GENERAL NOTE

For the reasons set out in the second paragraph of the General Note to the section, *supra*, para. [**37.1**], its entry into force before the entry date is not required—with the single exception provided for in this sub-s. (9).

ENTRY DATE

Sched. 1, Part II, Definition and Note.

EXCEPT TO AUTHORISE THE MAKING

At any time subsequent to enactment.

WITH EFFECT FROM (THE ENTRY DATE)

Though they may be made at any time subsequent to enactment (preceding comment) regulations under s. 435 cannot be made to take effect prior to 1st January 1973. [**37.10**]

10. Restrictive trade practices

(1) Part I of the Restrictive Trade Practices Act 1956 shll apply to an agreement notwithstanding that it is or may be void by reason of any directly applicable Community provision, or is expressly authorised by or under any such provision; but the Restrictive Practices Court may decline or postpone the exercise of its jurisdiction under section 20 of the Act, or may (notwithstanding

section 22 (2)) exercise its jurisdiction under section 22, if and in so far as it appears to the court right so to do having regard to the operation of any such provision or to the purpose and effect of any authorisation or exemption granted in relation thereto, and the Registrar may refrain from taking proceedings before the court in respect of any agreement if and for so long as he thinks it appropriate so to do having regard to the operation of any such provision and to the purpose and effect of any such authorisation or exemption.

(2) Regulations under section 19 of the Restrictive Trade Practices Act 1956 may require that the Registrar shall be furnished in respect of an agreement with information as to any steps taken, or decision given, under or for the purpose of any directly applicable Community provision affecting the agreement, and that the information so given or such part, if any of it, as may be provided by the regulations shall be included in the particulars to be entered or filed in the register under section 11 (2); but an agreement shall be exempt from registration under the Act so long as there is in force in relation thereto any authorisation given for the purpose of any provision of the E.C.S.C. Treaty relating to restrictive trade practices.

(3) At the end of section 33 (1) of the Restrictive Trade Practices Act 1956 (which restricts the disclosure of information obtained under the Act to the purposes there specified) there shall be added the words "or is made in pursuance of a Community obligation". [**38**]

GENERAL NOTE

The Treaties do not require that Community law relating to Restrictive Trade Practices be substituted for United Kingdom law on this subject. Indeed the concern of Community law here being essentially with trade in its *international* aspect as between member States, and with the maintenance of free competition within the Common Market on which the Communities are based, Community law could not in any event be a complete substitute for a system of law concerned with the prevention of restrictive trade practices purely in the *national* context and as demanded in the public interest of a single member State. But, though not substituted for United Kingdom law on this subject, Community law prevails over it, so that the effects of United Kingdom law must not be to authorise or condone trade agreements, or practices, which under Community law are unlawful. On the other hand, there is nothing in principle to prevent United Kingdom law from providing a more stringent control of restrictive trade practices than does Community law.

The main purpose of the section is consequently to ensure that United Kingdom law relating to restrictive trade practices shall not, after the entry date, operate in a manner incompatible with Community law. The section achieves that purpose, without amendment of the substantive provisions of the Restrictive Trade Practices Acts, merely by conferring discretion on the Restrictive Practices Court to decline or postpone the exercise of its jurisdiction, and on the Registrar, to refrain from taking proceedings before the Court, in certain circumstances. United Kingdom statutes relating to Monopolies and Mergers, being based on Ministerial discretion for their implementation, have not even been required to be referred to in the section.

A subsidiary purpose of the section is to facilitate the exercise by the Registrar of the discretion conferred on him for the main purpose. It is provided that information shall be furnished to him, as to any steps taken or decision given under Community law in respect of any agreement, in order that the Register may be completed by the addition of that information.

(Community instruments concerning Competition referred to in Art. 29 of the Act of Accession are listed in Annex I thereto—Cmnd. 4862—II, pp. 74–75; the instrument referred to in Art. 30 is in Annex II, *idem.* pp. 140–141; the one referred to in Art. 133 is in Annex VII, *idem*, p. 148). [**38.1**]

SUB-S. (1): GENERAL NOTE

The subsection makes provision in regard to the main purpose of the section described in the General Note, *supra*.

PART I OF THE RESTRICTIVE TRADE PRACTICES ACT 1956

This deals with the "Registration and Judicial Investigation of Restrictive Trading Agreements".

SHALL APPLY

Unless the 1956 Act had been repealed it would be bound to apply. Consequently the first four lines of the subsection may be considered merely declaratory. It is implicit in the subsection, however, that it shall apply in relation with the European Communities Act, only on and after the entry date (Sched. 1, Part II, ENTRY DATE, Definition and Note) because, prior to that date, no "directly applicable Community provision" can take effect in the United Kingdom (Sched. 1, Part II, COMMUNITY OBLIGATION, Definition and Note; "directly applicable". Introduction, para. [**16**] *ante*.).

(It was not on the basis that Community law could be "directly applicable" in a non-member State that the European Court held, before the enactment of the present Act, that the European Commission had lawfully imposed fines on a United Kingdom company and companies in another non-member State, for participating in a restrictive agreement contrary to Community law and taking effect within the Community; it was on the basis that the Company had acted through its subsidiary company incorporated in a member State and that the agreement containing the restriction had taken effect within the Community). [**38.2**]

IS OR MAY BE VOID . . . OR IS EXPRESSLY AUTHORISED

See, *for example*, as to "is or may be void", agreements "automatically void" by virtue of the E.E.C. Treaty, Art. 85 (1) and (2); and (3) as to declaration of the inapplicability of (1) and (2) to certain types of agreements and practices

See, *for example*, as to "expressly authorised", the E.C.S.C. Treaty, Arts. 65 and 66.

Whether void or authorised by or under any directly applicable Community provision (see next comment) an agreement remains subject to Part I of the Restrictive Trade Practices Act 1956. But no proceedings thereunder, or under any other enactment, can validate an agreement *void* under any directly applicable Community provision—precisely because it *is* directly applicable in the United Kingdom. On the other hand there is no legal obstacle to prevent an agreement expressly *authorised* under Community law from being invalidated under United Kingdom law, or to prevent separate proceedings under United Kingdom law in respect of an agreement declared void under Community law. [**38.3**]

DIRECTLY APPLICABLE COMMUNITY PROVISION

As to "directly applicable" see Sched. 1, Part II, COMMUNITY OBLIGATION, Definition and Note; Introduction, para. [**16**], *ante*).

THE RESTRICTIVE PRACTICES COURT MAY DECLINE OR POSTPONE . . . THE REGISTRAR MAY REFRAIN

On and after the entry date (see SHALL APPLY, *supra*) proceedings under Part I of the Restrictive Trade Practices Act 1956 may become pointless in respect of an agreement that is *void* by reason of a directly applicable Community provision; and, in respect of an agreement that *may be void* by reason of such a provision, proceedings under the Act may be undesirable until so-called "negative clearance" by the European Commission has been secured for it, or pointless if and when "negative clearance" is refused.

The above provisions of the subsection confer on the Court and the Registrar the discretion necessary to enable them to avoid pointless or undesirable proceedings of this kind and to ensure the compatibility with Community law of the implementation of United Kingdom law. But, though the court "may decline or postpone the exercise of its jurisdiction under s. 20 of the Act . . . having regard to the . . . purpose and effect of any authorization or exemption granted in relation" to any directly applicable Community provision, and the Registrar similarly may refrain from taking proceedings, there is no legal obstacle to prevent proceedings under Part I of the Restrictive Practices Act 1956 in respect of an agreement *expressly authorised* in Community law (IS OR MAY BE VOID . . . OR IS EXPRESSLY AUTHORISED, *supra*) nor to separate proceedings under United Kingdom law in respect of an agreement declared void under Community law. [**38.4**]

ITS JURISDICTION UNDER SECTION 20 OF THE ACT

The section makes provision as to the jurisdiction and powers of the Court. It has "jurisdiction . . . to declare whether or not any restrictions by virtue of which" Part I of the Act applies to an agreement are contrary to the public interest. If it finds any such restrictions to be contrary to the public interest "the agreement shall be void in respect of those restrictions", and the Court may "upon the application of the Registrar, make such order as appears to the Court to be proper for restraining all or any of the persons party to the agreement who carry on business in the United Kingdom—(*a*) from giving effect to or enforcing or purporting to enforce, the agreement in respect of those restrictions; (*b*) from making any other agreement (whether with the same parties or with other parties) to the like effect". [**38.5**]

EXERCISE ITS JURISDICTION UNDER SECTION 22 (NOTWITHSTANDING SECTION 22 (2)).

The words "notwithstanding section 22 (2)" in the present subsection remove the need for the Court to be satisfied of any one or more of the seven circumstances set out in s. 21 of the 1956 Act, in the absence of which satisfaction, "a restriction accepted in pursuance of any agreement shall be deemed to be contrary to the public interest . . ."

Under s. 22 (1) the Court may "discharge any previous declaration . . . in respect of any restriction and any order made by the Court in pursuance thereof and substitute such other declaration, and make such order in pursuance thereof, as appears to the Court to be proper . . ."

S. 22 (2) makes the provisions of s. 21 apply, with the necessary modifications in relation to proceedings under s. 22, as they apply in relation to proceedings under s. 20 (as to which see preceding comment). S. 21 provides that ". . . a restriction accepted in pursuance of any agreement shall be deemed to be contrary to the public interest unless the Court is satisfied of any one or more of the following circumstances" (which are seven in number). [**38.6**]

SUB-S. (2): GENERAL NOTE

The subsection makes provision in regard to the subsidiary purpose of the section described in the General Note, *supra*.

REGULATIONS UNDER SECTION 19 (OF THE 1956 ACT)

S. 19 empowers the Registrar to make, by statutory instrument, "regulations for purposes of registration under Part I of this Act and for purposes connected therewith" particularly in regard to the furnishing of particulars, information and documents, or to the prescribing the form of any notice, certificate or other document, or to regulating the inspection of the register or any document kept by the Registrar.

ANY STEPS TAKEN

That is, only "steps taken under or for the purpose of any directly applicable Community provision . . ."

For example, notification of the agreement to the European Commission to obtain negative clearance in respect of Community free-competition provisions, or a communication regarding the contents of an agreement from the European Commission to a party or parties to the agreement, in the United Kingdom. (It is the practice of the European Commission to keep member States informed of the steps exemplified in this note.)

Steps taken by the parties as between themselves, without reference to the European Commission, to amend an agreement so as to avoid its being caught by any directly applicable Community provision might be held to be taken "for the purpose of" such a provision. Information as to steps so taken in respect of an agreement registered under the Restrictive Trade Practices Act 1956 must be furnished to the Registrar under existing regulations even if they are taken before the "entry date", and thus before any Community provision can become directly applicable. [**38.7**]

OR DECISION GIVEN

That is, only "given under or for the purpose of any directly applicable Community provision . . ." Cf. ANY STEPS TAKEN, *supra*.

For example, a decision of the European Commission in regard to negative clearance of the agreement in respect of Community free competition provisions. As a matter of construction, a "decision *given*" does not embrace a decision *taken* by the parties to the agreement. [**38.8**]

DIRECTLY APPLICABLE COMMUNITY PROVISION

Prior to the entry date no "directly applicable Community provision" can take effect in the United Kingdom (see, under sub.s (1) SHALL APPLY, and DIRECTLY APPLICABLE COMMUNITY PROVISION: Sched. 1, Part II, "Community obligation, Definition and Note; Introduction, para. [**16**], *ante*).

AUTHORISATION . . . FOR THE PURPOSE OF . . . THE E.C.S.C. TREATY

The E.C.S.C. Treaty provides for the authorisation by the High Authority (now the Commission, by virtue of Art. 9 of the Brussels Treaty of 8th April 1965 establishing a single Council and a single Commission of the European Communities (see Sched. 1, Part I, 5)) under *Art. 65*, of "specialisation agreements or joint-buying or joint-sellling agreements in respect of particular products", subject to certain findings, and under *Art. 66*, of a concentration between undertakings (engaged in production in the coal or the steel industry) one of which at least is in the European territories of the member States or any European territory for whose external relations a member State is responsible, if the concentration is itself within those territories. [**38.9**]

SECTION 33 (1) OF THE RESTRICTIVE TRADE PRACTICES ACT 1956

This, as amended, provides:

> "**33** (1) No information with respect to any particular trade or business which has been obtained under or by virtue of this Act shall, so long as that trade or business continues to be carried on, be disclosed without the consent of the person for the time being carrying on that trade or business, unless the disclosure is for the purpose of facilitating the performance of any functions of the Board of Trade or the Registrar under this Act, or under the Monopolies and Restrictive Practices (Inquiry and Control) Act 1948, or for the purposes of, or of any report of, any proceedings before the Restrictive Practices Court or any other legal proceedings, whether civil or criminal, under this Act or arising out of the carrying of this Act into effect, *or is made in pursuance of a Community obligation.*"

As to "Community obligation" see Sched. 1, Part II, Definition and Note. [**38.10**]

11. Community offences

(1) A person who, in sworn evidence before the European Court, makes any statement which he knows to be false or does not believe to be true shall, whether he is a British subject or not, be guilty of an offence and may be proceeded against and punished—

(*a*) in England and Wales as for an offence against section 1 (1) of the Perjury Act 1911; or

(*b*) in Scotland for an offence against section 1 of the False Oaths (Scotland) Act 1933; or

(*c*) in Northern Ireland as for an offence against section 1 (1) of the Perjury Act (Northern Ireland) 1946.

Where a report is made as to any such offence under the authority of the European Court, then a bill of indictment for the offence may, in England or Wales or in Northern Ireland, be preferred as in a case where a prosecution is ordered under section 9 of the Perjury Act 1911 or section 8 of the Perjury Act (Northern Ireland) 1946, but the report shall not be given in evidence on a person's trial for the offence.

(2) Where a person (whether a British subject or not) owing either—

(*a*) to his duties as a member of any Euratom institution or committee, or as an officer or servant of Euratom; or

(*b*) to his dealings in any capacity (official or unofficial) with any Euratom institution or installation or with any Euratom joint enterprise;

has occasion to acquire, or obtain cognisance of, any classified information, he shall be guilty of a misdemeanour if, knowing or having reason to believe that it is classified information, he communicates it to any unauthorised person or makes any public disclosure of it, whether in the United Kingdom or elsewhere and whether before or after the termination of those duties or dealings; and for this purpose "classified information" means any facts, information, knowledge, documents or objects that are subject to the security rules of a member State or of any Euratom institution.

This subsection shall be construed, and the official Secrets Act 1911 to 1939 shall have effect, as if this subsection were contained in the Official Secrets Act 1911, but so that in that Act sections 10 and 11, except section 10 (4), shall not apply.

(3) This section shall not come into force until the entry date. [**39**]

GENERAL NOTE

Two types of Community offence are covered by the section: (i) Perjury, in proceedings before the European Court, by any person, whether a British subject or not, and (ii) communication, by any person whether a British subject or not, of Euratom "classified information" to any unauthorised person, or public disclosure thereof. In view of the legal nature of the Communities, no provision is possible for prosecution in respect of either type of offence directly under Community law itself. It has consequently been made a Community obligation that member States should provide for such prosecution as a matter of their respective national and domestic laws. The section does not come into force until the entry date; it applies to any person, whether a British subject or not. [**39.1**]

SUB-S. (1): GENERAL NOTE

The subsection makes provision in respect of perjury in proceedings before the European Court. It does not come into force until the entry date (sub-s. 3).

IN SWORN EVIDENCE

For clarification of the meaning of "sworn" see Perjury Act 1911, s. 15, and Perjury Act (Northern Ireland) 1946, s. 15.

The protocols on the Statute of the European Court annexed respectively to the Economic Community Treaty (Art. 25) and to the Euratom Treaty (Art. 26) provide in identical terms: "Witness and experts may be heard on oath taken in the form laid down in the rules of procedure or in the manner laid down by the law of the country of the witness or expert. The Court may order that a witness or expert be heard by the judicial authority of his place of permanent residence . . . ." The corresponding provision of the Coal and Steel Community protocol (in Art. 28) provides: "Des témoins peuvent être entendus dans les conditions qui seront déterminées par le règlement de procédure. Ils peuvent être entendus sous la foi du serment."

Rule 47 of the Rules of Procedure of the European Court provides:

Paragraph 4. After verification of the identity of the witnesses, the President shall inform them that they will be required to certify their statements on oath . . .

Paragraph 5. After giving evidence, the witness shall take the following oath: "I swear that what I have said is the truth, the whole truth and nothing but the truth".

The oath may be taken in manner laid down by the law of the country of the witness concerned.

The Court may, with the agreement of the parties, excuse the witness from being sworn.

Paragraph 6. Under the President's direction, the Registrar shall draw up a record of each witness's evidence. After being read out this record shall be signed by the witness, the President or Judge acting as Rapporteur and the Registrar. It shall constitute an official record." [**39.2**]

SHALL, WHETHER . . . A BRITISH SUBJECT OR NOT, BE GUILTY OF AN OFFENCE

The words are necessary to convert an offence under Community law into an offence under United Kingdom law, so that provision for prosecution may be made under the latter (this is done by the following clause: "may be proceeded against and punished— (*a*) . . . (*b*) . . . (*c*) . . ."). The effect of the words is to make committal proceedings unnecessary and to enable the Director of Public Prosecutions, or in Scotland the Procurator Fiscal, to prefer an indictment forthwith.

PROCEEDED AGAINST AND PUNISHED

The Community legal order does not (and by its nature, cannot) contain provision for such proceedings of its own. They must therefore be taken in accordance with the national laws of the member States, and to take them is a Community obligation of member States. The protocols on the Statute of the European Court annexed respectively to the Economic Community Treaty (Art. 27) and to the Euratom Treaty

(Art. 28), provide in identical terms: "A member State shall treat any violation of an oath by a witness or an expert in the same manner, as if the offence had been committed before one of its courts with jurisdiction in civil proceedings. At the instance of the Court, the member State concerned shall prosecute the offender before its competent Court." The corresponding provision (Art. 28) in the protocol on the Statute of the Court annexed to the Coal and Steel Community Treaty reads: "Lorsqu'il est établi qu'un témoin ou un expert a dissimulé ou contrefait la réalité des faits sur lesquels il a déposé ou été interrogé par la Cour, celle-ci est habilitée à saisir de ce manquement le ministre de la Justice de l'État dont le témoin ou l'expert est ressortissant, en vue de lui voir appliquer les sanctions prévues dans chaque cas par sa loi nationale." (In similar manner, enforcement of judgments of the European Court, and of "decisions of the Council or of the Comission which impose a pecuniary obligation on persons other than States . . . shall be governed by the rules of civil procedure in force in the States in the territory of which it is carried out . . ." E.C. Treaty, Article 192). **[39.3]**

REPORT . . . UNDER THE AUTHORITY OF THE EUROPEAN COURT

The purpose of the provision contained in the final paragraph of the subsection (beginning at "Where a report . . .") is to place a report of the European Court on the same footing as a report from an English or Northern Irish judge. (Perjury Act 1911, s. 9 and Perjury Act (Northern Ireland) 1946, s. 8) which may direct a prosecution for perjury. Such a direction obviates the necessity for the usual committal proceedings—see Administration of Justice (Miscellaneous Provisions) Act 1933, s. 2 (2) (*b*) and Grand Jury (Abolition) Act (Northern Ireland) 1969, s. 2 (2) (*d*).

The Supplementary Rules of Procedure of the European Court provide (in Art. 6): "The Court, after hearing the Advocate General, may decide to report to the Minister of Justice of the Member State within the jurisdiction of whose courts criminal proceedings fall to be taken, any false evidence given by a witness, or any false statement made by an expert, on oath before the Court", and (in Art. 7): "The Registrar shall be responsible for transmitting the decision of the Court. Such decision shall set out the facts and circumstances on which the report is founded". The authority in Community law for these Supplementary Rules of Procedure derives in the first place from Art. 109 of the Rules of Procedure. Ultimately it derives from the approval of the Council of Ministers in accordance with the Treaties establishing respectively the Economic Community (Art. 188) and Euratom (Art. 160), which provide in identical terms: "The Court of Justice shall adopt its rules of procedure. These shall require the unanimous approval of the Council" *or*, in the case of the Coal and Steel Community, it derives from Art. 44 of the Protocol on the Statute of the Court, annexed to the Treaty: "La Cour établit elle-même son règlement de procédure . . ."

For the purposes of Art. 6 of the Court's Supplementary Rules of Procedure quoted above, the question as to which United Kingdom Ministers are to be regarded as "the Minister of Justice" is for the decision of the United Kingdom government. **[39.4]**

SHALL NOT BE GIVEN IN EVIDENCE

The result is that proof of the offence must be established by the normal means available in United Kingdom law.

The effect of the words is that such a report by the European Court is not within the provision as to evidence of s. 3 (3), is not within the expression there used: "including any judgment or order of the European Court", and is not within the meaning of "Community instrument" (s. 3 (3) and (4)).

SUB-S. (2): GENERAL NOTE

The subsection makes provision in respect of the communication of "classified information" of Euratom to any unauthorised person, or the public disclosure of it, anywhere, by any person whether a British subject or not. The subsection does not come into force until the entry date (sub-s. 3). It implements, though not expressed so to do, Euratom Regulation No. 3 made by virtue of Art. 24 of the Euratom Treaty. (Arts. 14 and 15 of that Regulation make provision as to authorisations). See also Euratom Treaty, Art. 194. **[39.5]**

EURATOM INSTITUTION OR COMMITTEE

Definition "Community Institution", Sched. 1, Part II, and Note. The wording of (*a*) in the subsection removes all uncertainty, as the definition does not, which Community organs are included in the expression "Institution". The four Euratom Institutions—using the expression in the strict sense to mean those which are empowered to make acts that are binding in Community law—are The (parliamentary) Assembly, the Council, the Commission and the Court of Justice. Euratom has two Committees, both with advisory status: the Economic and Social Committee (which must be consulted by the Council or the Commission where the Treaty so provides) and the Scientific and Technical Committee, attached by the Treaty to the Commission. [**39.6**]

OWING . . . (*b*) TO HIS DEALINGS

The wording of (*b*) appears to omit dealings with a Euratom *committee* (see *supra*, EURATOM INSTITUTION OR COMMITTEE), unless the definition of "Community Institution" in Sched. 1, Part II (see Note) must be read as including committees.

SHALL BE GUILTY OF A MISDEMEANOUR

These words are necessary to convert an offence under Community law into an offence under United Kingdom law, so that provision may be made for prosecution under the latter.

SECURITY RULES

See Euratom Council Regulation No. 3 made under Art. 24 of the Euratom Treaty. Security rules comparable to those of the United Kingdom exist in some other member States.

SUB-S. (3): ENTRY DATE

Sched. **1**, Part II, Definition and Note. [**39.7**]

12. Furnishing of information to Communities

Estimates, returns and information that may under section 9 of the Statistics of Trade Act 1947 or section 80 of the Agriculture Act 1947 be disclosed to a government department or Minister in charge of a government department may, in like manner, be disclosed in pursuance of a Community obligation to a Community institution. [**40**]

GENERAL NOTE

This section makes provision as to disclosure of information to a Community institution in pursuance of a Community obligation.

COMMUNITY OBLIGATION

Sched. 1, Part II, Definition and Note.

COMMUNITY INSTITUTION

Sched. 1, Part II, Definition and Note. Cf. under s. 11 (3) EURATOM INSTITUTION OR COMMITTEE. Unless "Community institution" in the present subsection includes "Community committee" occasion might arise when it would not be lawful to make disclosure to a Community committee in accordance with an act of a Community institution requiring disclosure to be so made.

STATISTICS OF TRADE ACT 1947, S. 9 AND AGRICULTURE ACT 1947, S.80

These provide:

> "**9.** (1) No individual estimates or returns, and no information relating to an individual undertaking, obtained under the foregoing provisions of this Act, shall without the consent in writing of the person carrying on the undertaking which is the subject of the estimates, returns or information be disclosed except—
>
> (*a*) in accordance with directions given by the Minister in charge of the government department in possession of the estimates, returns of information to a Government department or to the Import Duties Advisory Committee for the purposes of the exercise by that department or Committee of any of their functions;
>
> (*b*) for the purposes of any proceedings for an offence under this Act or any report of those proceedings.
>
> (2) If any information to be obtained for the purposes of a census under this Act is also obtainable under any other enactment which restricts the disclosure of information obtained thereunder, and the Board of Trade are of opinion that similar restrictions should be applied to any information to be obtained for the purposes of the census, the Board shall by order provide for the application, without modifications or with such adaptations or modifications as the Board think fit, of those restrictions to the information to be so obtained, or any part thereof, in addition to the restrictions imposed by this section.

(3) Without prejudice to the provisions of the last foregoing subsection, if it appears to the Board of Trade that—

(*a*) the nature of the information to be obtained for the purposes of a census under this Act, or

(*b*) the nature of the undertakings to be covered by the census,

would make it desirable to impose restrictions on the disclosure of information obtained by means of the census additional to the restrictions imposed by this section, the Board of Trade may by order prohibit the disclosure of information relating to particular undertakings obtained by means of the census, or any part of that information, except to such persons or for such purposes as may be specified in the order.

(4) No order shall be made under this section unless a draft thereof has been laid before Parliament and has been approved by resolution of each House of Parliament.

(5) The following provisions shall have effect with respect to any report summary or other communication to the public of information obtained under the foregoing provisions of this Act—

(*a*) no such report, summary or communication shall disclose the number of returns received with respect to the production of any article if that number is less than five;

(*b*) in compiling any such report, summary or communication the competent authority shall so arrange it as to prevent any particulars published therein from being identified as being particulars relating to any individual person or undertaking except with the previous consent in writing of that person or the person carrying on that undertaking, as the case may be—but this provision shall not prevent the disclosure of the total quantity or value of any articles produced, sold or delivered; so, however, that before disclosing any such total the competent authority shall have regard to any representations made to them by any person who alleges that the disclosure thereof would enable particulars relating to him or to an undertaking carried on by him to be deduced from the total disclosed.

(6) If any person discloses any individual estimates or returns or any information contrary to the provisions of this section, or of any order made under this section, he shall be liable, on summary conviction, to imprisonment for a term not exceeding three months or to a fine not exceeding fifty pounds, or on conviction on indictment to imprisonment for a term not exceeding two years or to a fine not exceeding five hundred pounds, or, in either case, to both such imprisonment and such a fine.

80. No information relating to any particular land or business being information which has been obtained under section seventy-eight or seventy-nine of this Act. shall be published or otherwise disclosed without the previous consent in writing of the person by whom the information was furnished and every other person whose interest may in the opinion of the Minister be affected by the disclosure, being an owner or the occupier of the land:

Provided that nothing in this section shall restrict the disclosure of information—

(*a*) to the Minister in charge of any Government department, to any authority acting under an enactment for regulating the marketing of any agricultural produce, or to any person exercising functions on behalf of any such Minister or authority for the purpose of the exercise of those functions;

(*b*) to an authority having power under any enactment to give permission for the development of land for the purpose of assisting that authority in the preparation of proposals relating to such development or in considering whether or not to give such permission;

(*c*) if the disclosure is confined to situation, extent, number and kind of livestock, character of land and name and address of owner and occupier to any person to whom the Minister considers that the disclosure thereof is required in the public interest;

(*d*) to any person for the purposes of any criminal proceedings under the next following section or for the purposes of any report of such proceedings,

or the use of information in any manner which the Minister thinks necessary or expedient in connection with the maintenance of the supply of food in the United Kingdom." [**40.1**]

SCHEDULES

SCHEDULE 1

DEFINITIONS RELATING TO COMMUNITIES

PART I

THE PRE-ACCESSION TREATIES

Section 1

1. The "E.C.S.C. Treaty", that is to say, the Treaty establishing the European Coal and Steel Community, signed at Paris on the 18th April 1951. **[41]**

2. The "E.E.C. Treaty", that is to say, the Treaty establishing the European Economic Community, signed at Rome on the 25th March 1957. **[42]**

(3) The "Euratom Treaty", that is to say, the Treaty establishing the European Atomic Energy Community, signed at Rome on the 25th March 1957. **[43]**

4. The Convention on certain Institutions common to the European Communities, signed at Rome on the 25th March 1957. **[44]**

5. The Treaty establishing a single Council and a single Commission of the European Communities, signed at Brussels on the 8th April 1965. **[45]**

6. The Treaty amending certain Budgetary Provisions of the Treaties establishing the European Communities and of the Treaty establishing a single Council and a single Commission of the European Communities, signed at Luxembourg on the 22nd April 1970. **[46]**

7. Any treaty entered into before the 22nd January 1972 by any of the Communities (with or without any of the member States) or, as a treaty ancillary to any treaty included in this Part of this Schedule, by the member States (with or without any other country). **[47]**

PART II

OTHER DEFINITIONS

"Economic Community", "Coal and Steel Community" and "Euratom" mean respectively the European Economic Community, the European Coal and Steel Community and the European Atomic Energy Community. **[48]**

"Community customs duty" means, in relation to any goods, such duty of customs as may from time to time be fixed for those goods by directly applicable Community provision as the duty chargeable on importation into member States. **[49]**

COMMUNITY CUSTOMS DUTY

Community customs duties are "fixed" (s. 5 (1)) at intervals, "in relation to" different categories of goods, by a provision that is "directly applicable" (see Introduction, para. **[16]** *ante*) in all member States. Being "directly applicable" such a provision must, in accordance with s. 2 (1), "without further enactment" be recognised and available in law in the United Kingdom. But inasmuch as the Community provision merely "fixes" the duty, making it chargeable without in fact charging it, the charge is imposed, as a matter of United Kingdom law, by virtue of s. 5.

"Community institution" means any institution of any of the Communities or common to the Communities; and any reference to an institution of a particular Community shall include one common to the Communities when it acts for that Community, and similarly with references to a committee, officer or servant of a particular Community. **[50]**

COMMUNITY INSTITUTION

There is possibly room for doubt whether or not "Community institution" includes a Community committee.

On the one hand, the implication of the words "when it acts for that Community" seems to be that only an institution empowered to make an act that is binding in Community law (namely, a COMMUNITY INSTRUMENT, see *infra*) is within the definition, which therefore includes only (i) the (parliamentary) Assembly, (ii) the Council, (iii) the Commission and (iv) the Court of Justice. (Though a report as to perjury made under the authority of the Court (s. 11 (1)) is not a Community instrument for the purposes of s. 3 (3) or (4)). The remaining words in the definition also imply a distinction between institution and committee. The following definition "Community instrument" lends some further weight to this, because a Community committee (which may "submit its opinion", *e.g.*, Euratom Treaty, Art. 170) does not issue what would usually be "an instrument" (cf. "statutory instrument").

On the other hand in the Act of Accession, Part Two (Adjustment to the Treaties), Title I (provisions governing the Institutions) consists of seven chapters, the first four of which make provision respectively in regard to the four institutions listed above, but the last three of which make provision respectively in regard to (i) the Economic and Social Council (of E.E.C. and Euratom), (ii) the E.C.S.C. Consultative Committee, (iii) the Scientific and Technical Committee (of Euratom). (The Economic and Social Committee is similarly, in the treaties originally establishing respectively the Economic Community and Euratom, provided for under the same Title as the four institutions listed above. The E.C.S.C. Consultative Committee "attached to the High Authority" (now the Commission) is established by virtue of an article in the Chapter making provision for the High Authority, contained in a title of only four chapters concerned respectively with the four institutions listed above. The Scientific and Technical Committee of Euratom is set up and "attached to the Commission" by virtue of an article, in the original Euratom Treaty, similarly contained in a chapter making provision for the Commission.

"Community instrument" means any instrument issued by a Community institution. [**51**]

COMMUNITY INSTRUMENT

See COMMUNITY INSTITUTION, *supra*.

The expression "Community instrument" certainly includes the acts, binding in Community law, that may be made by the (parliamentary) Assembly, the Council, the Commission, or the Court of Justice. All such acts accord with the connotation of "instrument" both in English, linguistically, and as a matter of United Kingdom law—the Interpretation Act, ss. 31 and 37, contain the following: ". . . to make, grant, or issue any *instrument*, that is to say, any Order in Council, order, warrant, scheme, letter patent, rules, regulations, or bylaws . . ."

But the Recommendations and Opinions of the Council and Commission of Euratom and of the E.E.C. "shall have no binding force" (E.E.C. Treaty, Art. 189, E.A.E.C. Treaty, Art. 161) nor have the opinions of the E.C.S.C. High Authority (E.C.S.C. Treaty Art. 14). Is any one of these a "Community instrument" or is it some "other act" as distinguished from an instrument by s. 3 (2) (and nowhere else) in the present Act? And are the acts of a Community Committee (as referred to, for example, in s. 11) "instruments", or "other acts" within the meaning of s. 3 (2), or not within that meaning because "Institution" does not include "Committee"?

"Community obligation" means any obligation created or arising by or under the Treaties, whether an enforceable Community obligation or not. [**52**]

COMMUNITY OBLIGATION

The wording of the definition follows that of s. 2 (1), and the expression, being similar to ENFORCEABLE COMMUNITY RIGHT (*infra*) also falls to be construed in accordance therewith. Thus, a Community obligation may come into existence in any of the following four ways:— being (i) created by, or (ii) created under, or (iii) arising by, or (iv) arising under, the Treaties (as defined in s. 1 (2)).

The words "enforceable Community obligation" in the definition clearly refer to enforceability in United Kingdom law, at the suit, maybe, of private parties, as provided in s. 2 (1). But, by the definition, "Community obligation" also includes an obligation which is not *per se* enforceable by virtue of s. 2 (1), such as any Community obligation of the United Kingdom. A Community obligation *of the United Kingdom* may be an obligation to implement in or for the United Kingdom (under s. 2 (2) (*a*)) a provision of Community law that is *not*, in the eyes of that law, "directly applicable". Or, a Community obligation of the United Kingdom may arise in relation to s. 2 (1) to take, as a matter of United Kingdom law, measures that are necessary to ensure that a directly applicable Community provision (*e.g.* a Regulation; and see under s. 2 (1) WITHOUT FURTHER ENACTMENT) takes its full effect under United Kingdom law. S. 2 (2) (*b*), by the words "or the operation from time to time of sub-s. (1)", enables this to be done by Order in Council or regulations.

Community obligations of the United Kingdom arising in either of the two ways illustrated in the preceding paragraph can exist only in and by virtue of Community law; they are obligations, to the particular Community under the law of which they arise, owed by the United Kingdom, as a member State, to that Community. The sanctions that exist in the event of their non-fulfilment are those provided by Community Law (see E.E.C. Treaty, Arts. 169–171; Euratom Treaty, Arts. 141–143; E.C.S.C. Treaty, Arts. 88–89). In United Kingdom law there exists as from the entry date, not a sanction, but a remedy for non-fulfilment by the United Kingdom of its obligation to take necessary measures to give effect to directly applicable Community provisions; for the constant case law of the European Court (note s. 3 (1)) is to the effect that, in certain circumstances, Courts and tribunals of member States must nevertheless order that they be given effect to.

There may be some ground for thinking that a Community obligation of the United Kingdom arising in relation to s. 2 (1) may be considered fulfilled as a matter of Community law if effect is given solely to the *result* it seeks. But if the words in s. 2 (1), "shall be recognised and available in law", can be read as mandatory—so that United Kingdom authorities have a duty under the subsection to make "all such rights, etc." available in law, such a duty could not properly be described as a Community obligation of the United Kingdom; it would be a duty, under United Kingdom law, related to a Community obligation.

"Enforceable Community right" and similar expressions shall be construed in accordance with section 2 (1) of this Act. [**53**]

ENFORCEABLE COMMUNITY RIGHT

This expression, construed as required in accordance with s. 2 (1), can include only Community rights enforceable *in* United Kingdom law on the basis of their being founded in "directly applicable" Community law (see Introduction, para. [**16**] *et seq.*, *ante*). The expression obviously does not include any right of the United Kingdom *vis-à-vis* the Communities since the enforceability of such rests on Community (and, possibly, international) law, and not on United Kingdom law.

"Community obligation" (*supra*) must be regarded as a "similar expression" to "enforceable Community right".

"Entry date" means the date on which the United Kingdom becomes a member of the Communities. [**54**]

ENTRY DATE

The Treaty of Accession ("concerning the accession . . . Denmark, Ireland, Norway and the United Kingdom to the European Economic Community and the European Atomic Energy Committee" signed on 22nd January 1972) provides in Art. 1 that these countries "hereby become members" of these two Communities, and in Art. 2 that "This Treaty will enter into force on 1st January 1973 provided that all the instruments of ratification have been deposited on that date". The instruments of ratification", or, alternatively, accession, here referred to, are such instruments deposited by all *ten* of the High Contracting Parties, that is, the original six member States of the Communities and the four acceding States mentioned above. Art. 2 of the Treaty, however, also provides that where the *four* acceding States "have not all deposited their instruments of ratification and accession in due time, the Treaty shall enter into force for those States which have deposited their instruments"—provided, it appears necessarily to be implied, that the original six member States have deposited their instruments of ratification in the manner prescribed in the first two sentences of Art. 2. Accession of the four acceding States to the European Coal and Steel Community is effected by the Decision of the Council of the European Communities of 22nd January 1972, which provides that they "may become members" thereof "by acceding, under the conditions laid down in this Decision, to the Treaty establishing that Community, as amended or supplemented". Art. 2 of the Decision provides that "accession will take effect on 1st January 1973, "subject to provisoes, as to deposit of instruments of accession by the four States, equivalent to those contained in the Treaty of Accession to the other two Communities, quoted above.

Both the United Kingdom and Denmark ratified the Accession Treaty on 18th October 1972. Irish legislation envisaging ratification was before the Dail in late November 1972. Norway, as a result of a referendum which produced a vote against membership of the Communities, will not ratify the Treaty of Accession.

Ratifications by the six original member States are expected during December 1972.

"European Court" means the Court of Justice of the European Communities. **[55]**

EUROPEAN COURT

The present Court of Justice of the European Communities was first established by the Coal and Steel Treaty of 1951 as the judicial institution of the first European Community. In 1957, on the ratification of the Treaties establishing respectively the Economic Community and Euratom, it became the judicial institution of those Communities also. But though there is, as a result, a single Court for all three Communities, the jurisdiction it exercises—and to some extent its procedure—varies according to the Community in respect of the law of which the Court adjudicates in any given case.

"Member", in the expression "member State", refers to membership of the Communities. **[56]**

SCHEDULE 2

Section 2

PROVISIONS AS TO SUBORDINATE LEGISLATION

1.—(1) The powers conferred by section 2 (2) of this Act to make provision for the purposes mentioned in section 2 (2) (*a*) and (*b*) shall not include power—

(*a*) to make any provision imposing or increasing taxation; or

(*b*) to make any provision taking effect from a date earlier than that of the making of the instrument containing the provision; or

(*c*) to confer any power to legislate by means of orders, rules, regulations or other subordinate instrument, other than rules of procedure for any court or tribunal; or

(*d*) to create any new criminal offence punishable with imprisonment for more than two years or punishable on summary conviction with imprisonment for more than three months or with a fine of more than £400 (if not calculated on a daily basis) or with a fine of more than £5 a day.

(2) Sub-paragraph (1) (*c*) above shall not be taken to preclude the modification of a power to legislate conferred otherwise than under section 2 (2), or the extension of any such power to purposes of the like nature as those for which it was conferred; and a power to give directions as to matters of administration is not to be regarded as a power to legislate within the meaning of sub-paragraph (1) (*c*). **[57]**

2.—(1) Subject to paragraph 3 below, where a provision contained in any section of this Act confers power to make regulations (otherwise than by modification or extension of an existing power), the power shall be exercisable by statutory instrument.

(2) Any statutory instrument containing an Order in Council or regulations made in the exercise of a power so conferred, if made without a draft having been approved by resolution of each House of Parliament, shall be subject to annulment in pursuance of a resolution of either House. **[58]**

3. Nothing in paragraph 2 above shall apply to any Order in Council made by the Governor of Northern Ireland or to any regulations made by a Minister or department of the Government of Northern Ireland; but where a provision contained in any section of this Act confers power to make such an Order in Council or regulations, then any Order in Council or regulations made in the exercise of that power,

if made without a draft having been approved by resolution of each House of the Parliament of Northern Ireland, shall be subject to negative resolution within the meaning of section 41 (6) of the Interpretation Act (Northern Ireland) 1954 as if the Order or regulations were a statutory instrument within the meaning of that Act. **[59]**

GENERAL NOTE

Cf. under s. 2 (4) POWERS CONFERRED . . . TO MAKE ORDERS IN COUNCIL AND REGULATIONS.

The Schedule consists of three paragraphs. Para. 1 is concerned essentially with the powers conferred by s. 2 (2) and defines, in sub-para. (1) (*a*) to (*d*), what is *excluded* from those powers. Sub-para. (2) provides that the exclusion from those powers, by (1) (*c*), of power "to confer any power to legislate by means of orders, rules, regulations or other subordinate instrument, other than rules of procedure for any court or tribunal" is not to "be taken to preclude the modification of a power to legislate conferred *otherwise* than under s. 2 (2), or the extension of any such power to purposes of the like nature as those for which it was conferred". Sub-para. (2) also provides that "a power to give directions as to matters of administration is not to be regarded as a power to legislate within the meaning of sub-para. (1) (*c*)".

Paragraph 2 (1) requires a power to make regulations conferred by *any* section of this Act to be exercised by statutory instrument—except where the power is conferred by modification or extension of an existing power. Para. 2 (2) provides that a draft of any statutory instrument made in accordance with sub-para. (1), as well as any statutory instrument containing an Order in Council, shall require approval of each House of Parliament or else be subject to annulment by resolution of either House.

Para. 3 makes particular provision for Northern Ireland in respect of the subject matter of para. 2. (In the same connection, comments relating to Northern Ireland, under ss. 2 (5), 4 (3) and 6 (2) (*b*), should be noted.)

SCHEDULE 3

Section 4

REPEALS

PART I

CUSTOMS TARIFF

Chapter	Short Title	Extent of Repeal
6 & 7 Eliz. 2 c. 6	The Import Duties Act 1958	The whole Act, except— section 4; Part II, including Schedules 3 to 5; in section 12 (4) the words "fish, whales or other natural produce of the sea, or goods produced or manufactured therefrom at sea, if brought direct to the United Kingdom, are", and paragraphs (*a*) and (*b*); and sections 13, 15 and 16 (1) and (2). In Part II, section 5 (2), (3), (5) and (6), section 7 (1) (*c*) with the preceding "and", section 9 (4) and section 9 (5) from "and" onwards. In Schedule 4, paragraph 1.
8 & 9 Eliz. 2 c. 19	The European Free Trade Association Act 1960	The whole Act.
1965 c. 65	The Finance Act 1965	Section 2, except subsection (5).

Chapter	Short Title	Extent of Repeal
1966 c. 18	The Finance Act 1966	In section 1, in subsection (1) the words between "1958" and "chargeable", and subsection (6). Section 9.
1969 c. 16	The Customs Duties (Dumping and Subsidies) Act 1969	The whole Act.
1971 c. 68	The Finance Act 1971	Section 1 (1) to (3).

The repeals in this Part of this Schedule shall take effect from such date as the Secretary of State may by order appoint.

PART II

SUGAR

Chapter	Short Title	Extent of Repeal
4 & 5 Eliz. 2 c. 48	The Sugar Act 1956	In section 3, subsection (1) from "including" onwards and subsection (2) (*b*). Section 4 (2) and (3). Section 5, except as regards advances made before this repeal takes effect. Sections 7 to 17. Section 18 (3) and (4). Sections 19 and 20. Sections 21 and 22, except as regards advances made and guarantees given before this repeal takes effect. Section 23, but without prejudice to the modification made by subsection (2) in the articles of association of the British Sugar Corporation. Sections 24 to 32. In section 33, in subsection (1) the words "regulations or", in subsection (2) the words from the beginning to "subsection", subsection (3) and subsection (5). In section 34, the words "or the Commissioners". In section 35, in subsection (2) all the definitions except those of "the Corporation", "financial year of the Sugar Board", "functions", "the Government", "home-grown beet" and "pension", in subsection

Chapter	Short Title	Extent of Repeal
4 & 5 Eliz. 2 c. 48 —*cont.*	The Sugar Act 1956—*cont.*	(3) the words "or of the Corporation" and subsections (4) to (7). Section 36 (2). In Schedule 3, paragraphs 2, 3 and 4. Schedule 4.
5 & 6 Eliz. 2 c. 57	The Agriculture Act 1957	Section 4. In section 36 (2) the words "and to sugar beet'.
10 & 11 Eliz. 2 c. 23	The South Africa Act 1962	In Schedule 2, paragraph 5.
10 & 11 Eliz. 2 c. 44	The Finance Act 1962	In section 3 (6) the words from "the Sugar Act 1956" onwards. Part II of Schedule 5.
1963 c. 11	The Agriculture (Miscellaneous Provisions) Act 1963	Section 25.
1964 c. 49	The Finance Act 1964	Section 22.
1966 c. 18	The Finance Act 1966	Section 52.
1968 c. 13	The National Loans Act 1968	In Schedule 2, the entry for the Sugar Act 1956, except as regards advances madeı before this repeal takes effect.
1968 c. 44	The Finance Act 1968	Section 58.

The repeals in this Part of this Schedule shall take effect from such date as the Minister of Agriculture, Fisheries and Food and the Secretary of State acting jointly may by order appoint.

PART III
SEEDS

Chapter	Short Title	Extent of Repeal
1964 c. 14	The Plant Varities and Seeds Act 1964	Section 5 (3). Sections 20 to 23A. Section 25 (8) (*b*) and the word "and" preceding it. Section 32. In section 34 (2) the words from "or in the Index" to "into force", and the words "or fact". Schedule 5.
1968 c. 29	The Trade Descriptions Act 1968	Section 2 (4) (*a*).
1968 c. 34	The Agriculture (Miscellaneous Provisions) Act 1968	Schedule 7, except amendments of section 1 of or Schedule 1 or 2 to the Plant Varieties and Seeds Act 1964.

The repeals in this Part of this Schedule shall take effect from such date as the Minister of Agriculture, Fisheries and Food and the Secretary of State acting jointly may by order appoint.

PART IV

MISCELLANEOUS

Chapter	Short Title	Extent of Repeal
9 & 10 Geo. 6 c. 59	The Coal Industry Nationalisation Act 1946	In section 4, in its application to the Industrial Coal Consumers' Council, subsections (1) to (8); and in its application to the Domestic Coal Consumers' Council, in subsection (2) the words "to represent the Board and", in subsection (3) (as applied by subsection (4)) the words from "and where" in paragraph (*a*) onwards and subsection (5). Section 4 (9), (10) and (11).
10 & 11 Geo. 6 c. 48	The Agriculture Act 1947	Section 2 (2).
15 & 16 Geo. 6 and 1 Eliz. 2 c. 44	The Customs and Excise Act 1952	Schedule 6, except for cases in which the value of goods falls to be determined as at a time before the entry date.
1 & 2 Eliz. 2 c. 15	The Iron and Steel Act 1953	Section 29.
5 & 6 Eliz. 2 c. 57	The Agriculture Act 1957	Section 2 (6) (*b*), with the preceding "or". Section 3. Section 8 (1), and in section 8 (2) the words "and subsection(1) of section 3". In section 11 the words "and 'special review'" and the words "or special review".
10 & 11 Eliz. 2 c. 22	The Coal Consumers' Councils (Northern Irish Interests) Act 1962	Section 1 (1) and (2), in so far as they apply to the Industrial Coal consumers' Council.
1963 c. 11	The Agriculture (Miscellaneous Provisions) Act 1963	Section 9 (8).
1967 c. 17	The Iron and Steel Act 1967	Sections 8, 15 and 30. Section 48 (2) (*b*). In Schedule 3, the entries relating to section 6 of the Iron and Steel Act 1949. In Schedule 4, section 6 of the Iron and Steel Act 1949 as there set out.
1967 c. 22	The Agriculture Act 1967	Section 61 (7). Section 64 (6). Section 65 (5).
1968 c. 48	The International Organisations Act 1968	Section 3. In section 4, the words "other than the Commission of the European Communities".
1970 c. 24	The Finance Act 1970	In Schedule 2, paragraph 5 (1) from "Where, by virtue" onwards, and paragraph 5 (2) (*b*) and (*c*), except for cases in which the value of goods falls to be determined as at a time before the entry date.
1970 c. 40	The Agriculture Act 1970	Section 106 (5).

SCHEDULE 4

Section 4

ENACTMENTS AMENDED

GENERAL NOTE

So far as appears desirable for convenience, an indication is given below of the relation of each amendment either to Community law or, as the case may be, to a section or sections of Part II of the Act.

Also, where it appears to facilitate reference, the texts of each amended section of certain Acts are set out in full below (with the amendments in italics) or a reference is given to the page in this work where the amended section is printed or a comment thereon is made.

A: *Customs Duties*

A (i): *Import Duty Reliefs etc.*

1.—(1) Save as provided by paragraphs (*a*) and (*b*) below, for the words "the Treasury", wherever occurring in Part II (including Schedule 3) of the Import Duties Act 1958, and for the words "the Board of Trade" or "the Board", wherever occurring in that Act or in section 1 of the Finance Act 1966, there shall be substituted the words "the Secretary of State" (and in section 6 (1) to (3) of the Act of 1958 and section 1 (1) (*a*) of that of 1966 there shall be made any consequential substitution of words in the singular for words in the plural); but in the Act of 1958—

(*a*) there shall be omitted section 5 (7), in section 8 (5) the words "on the recommendation of the Board of Trade", in section 9 (2) the words preceding the first "in" and the words "to recommend that" and in section 13 (4) the words "of the Treasury"; and

(*b*) for section 13 (1) there shall be substituted—

"(1) Any power to make orders which is conferred by this Act shall include power to vary or revoke any order made in the exercise of that power."

The coming into force of this sub-paragraph shall not affect the continuance in force of any order, regulations or direction previously made or given; but where any condition previously imposed under Part II of the Import Duties Act 1958 requires any consent of the Treasury or of the Board of Trade, it shall thereafter be construed as requiring instead that of the Secretary of State.

(2) In section 5 (4) of the Import Duties Act 1958 (power to provide by order for administration of any relief from duty under the section) after the words "any relief from duty under this section" there shall be inserted the words "or for the implementation or administration of any like relief provided for by any Community instrument", and after paragraph (*a*) there shall be inserted—

"(*aa*) where the relief is limited to a quota of imported goods, provide for determining the allocation of the quota or for enabling it to be determined by the issue of certificates or licences or otherwise;".

(3) In section 6 (1) of the Import Duties Act 1958 (power to exempt importations meant for research or other special purposes) before the words "any import duty" there shall be inserted the words "the whole or part of".

(4) In section 7 of the Import Duties Act 1958 (which confers power to exempt importations intended for export, but with power to attach conditions on the grant of exemption) there shall be added at the end of subsection (3) the words "or that, in such circumstances as the Commissioners may require, there shall be paid by way of duty such amount as may be so required"; and after subsection (3) there shall be inserted the following subsections:—

"(3A) For purposes of this section the Commissioners may treat any imported articles as if it were intended to re-export goods incorporating them or manufactured or produced from them, if the Commissioners are satisfied that goods incorporating, or manufactured or produced from, like articles have been or are intended to be exported and that in the circumstances it is proper for the imported articles to be so treated.

(3B) References in this section to goods manufactured or produced from any articles shall, in such cases and to such extent as the Commissioners may allow, be treated as including goods in the manufacture, production or repair of which those articles are used as an agent to carry out or facilitate any process or are used to treat, protect or test the goods or any component of them."

(5) In section 13 (4) of the Import Duties Act 1958 (orders lapsing unless approved by resolution of House of Commons) before the words "the statutory instrument" there shall be inserted the words "unless the order states that it does not do so otherwise than in pursuance of a Community obligation".

(6) In Schedule 3 to the Import Duties Act 1958 at the end of paragraph 8 (which allows relief under section 5 to be given with a view to conforming with international agreements) there shall be added at the end the words "or with a view to conforming with any Community obligations or otherwise affording relief provided for by or under the Community Treaties." [**61**]

CROSS REFERENCES

1—(1) See under s. 5 (3) para. [**33.11**], *ante*, and cf. s. 6 (5) (*b*).
For text of s. 13 Import Duties Act 1958, as amended, see para. [**33.12**], *ante*,
(2) For text of the amended s. 5 (4) of the Import Duties Act, see under s. 5, para. [**33.16**], *ante*.
(6) For text of the amended Schedule 3 to the Import Duties Act 1958, see under s. 5, para. [**33.16**], *ante*.

A(ii): *Customs and Excise Act* 1952

2.—(1) In the Customs and Excise Act 1952 there shall be made, with effect from the entry date, the amendments provided for by the following sub-paragraphs.

(2) In section 34, there shall be inserted after subsection (1) a new subsection—

"(1A) Where security for the payment of duty is given to the satisfaction of the Commissioners in accordance with such arrangements as may be prescribed by regulations of the Commissioners, then subject to such conditions as may be so prescribed or as the Commissioners may see fit to impose, the Commissioners may permit payment under this section of the duty to be deferred for such period as may be so prescribed, and duty of which payment is deferred under this subsection shall be deemed to have been paid for purposes of any relief from duty by way of drawback, for purposes of sections 35, 36 and 46 of this Act, and for such other purposes as may be so prescribed; but the regulations may provide for payment to be deferred in the case of some duties of customs or some goods but not of others";

and in section 86 (removal of warehoused goods) there shall be added at the end of subsection (4) the words "but section 34 (1A) of this Act shall apply to warehoused goods with the substitution of a reference to this section for any reference to that section".

AMENDED TEXT OF S. 34

S. 34 opens up the possibility for importers to receive the benefit of E.E.C. Directive 69/76 (which is concerned with the harmonisation of provisions for deferred payment of customs duties, charges having equivalent effect and agricultural levies). See also, s. 86, *infra*.

"**34.** (1) Save as permitted by or under this Act or any other enactment relating to customs, no imported goods shall be delivered or removed on importation until the importer has paid to the proper officer any duty chargeable thereon, and that duty shall in the case of goods of which entry is made be paid on making the entry.

(1A) *Where security for the payment of duty is given to the satisfaction of the Commissioners in accordance with such arrangements as may be prescribed by regulations of the Commissioners, then subject to such conditions as may be so prescribed or as the Commissioners may see fit to impose, the Commissioners may permit payment under this section of the duty to be deferred for such period as may be so prescribed, and duty of which payment is deferred under this subsection shall be deemed to have been paid for purposes of any relief from duty by way of drawback, for purposes of Sections* 35, 36 *and* 46 *of this Act, and for such other purposes as may be so prescribed; but the regulations may provide for payment to be deferred in the case of some duties of customs or some goods but not of others;*

(2) The duties of customs and the rates thereof chargeable on imported goods—

(*a*) if entry is made thereof, except where the entry is in the case of an entry by bill of sight, the perfect entry is for warehousing, shall be those in force with respect to such goods at the time of the delivery of the entry;
(*b*) if entry or, in the case of goods entered by bill of sight, perfect entry is made thereof for warehousing, shall be ascertained as provided in section eight-eight of this Act;
(*c*) if no entry is made thereof, shall be those in force with respect to such goods at the time of their importation.

(3) Any goods brought or coming into the United Kingdom by sea otherwise than as cargo, stores or baggage carried in a ship shall be chargeable with the like duty, if any, as would be applicable to those goods if they had been imported as merchandise; and if any question arises as to the origin of the goods they shall be deemed to be the produce of such country as the Commissioners may on investigation determine.

(4) Subject to the two next following sections and save as provided by or under any other enactment relating to customs any goods which are re-imported into the United Kingdom after exportation therefrom, whether they were manufactured or produced in or outside the United Kingdom and whether or not any duty was paid thereon at a previous importation, shall be treated for the purpose of charging duty in like manner as if they were being imported for the first time and, in the case of goods manufactured or produced in the United Kingdom, as if they had not been so manufactured or produced."

AMENDED TEXT OF S. 86

"**86.** (1) Before any goods are removed from warehouse the proprietor of the goods shall deliver to the proper officer an entry thereof in such form and manner containing such particulars as the Commissioners may direct.

(2) Subject to any provision of this or any other Act or of any instrument made thereunder as to the purposes for which any goods may be warehoused, goods may be entered under this section for any of the following purposes, that is to say

(*a*) for home use;
(*b*) for exportation;
(*c*) for use as stores;
(*d*) subject to such conditions and restrictions as the Commissioners see fit to impose, for removal to another warehouse approved for the warehousing of such goods;
(*e*) subject to such conditions and restrictions as aforesaid for removal for such other purposes, to such places and for such periods as the Commissioners may allow.

(3) Goods shall be deemed to have been duly entered under this section when the entry has been signed by the proper officer.

(4) Save as permitted by or under this Act, no goods shall be removed from a warehouse until any duty chargeable thereon has been paid, *but section 34 (1A) of this Act shall apply to warehoused goods with the substitution of a reference to this section for any reference to that section.*

(5) Warehoused goods shall not be removed from the warehouse or loaded into any ship, aircraft or vehicle for removal or for exportation or use as stores except with the authority of, and in accordance with any directions given by, the proper officer."

(3) At the end of section 67 there shall be added as a separate subsection (2)—

"(2) Without prejudice to subsection (1) above, where any question as to the duties of customs chargeable on any goods, or the operation of any prohibition or restriction on importation, depends on any question as to the place from which the goods were consigned, or any question where they or other goods are to be treated as grown, manufactured or produced, or any question as to payments made or relief from duty allowed in any country or territory, then—

(*a*) the Commissioners may require the importer of the goods to furnish to them, in such form as they may prescribe, proof of any statement made to them as to any fact necessary to determine that question, or of the accuracy of any certificate or other document furnished in connection with the importation of the goods and relating to the matter in issue, and if such proof is not furnished to their satisfaction, the question may be determined without regard to that statement or to that certificate or document; and

(*b*) if in any proceedings relating to the goods or to the duty chargeable thereon the accuracy of any such certificate or document comes in question, it shall be for the person relying on it to furnish proof of its accuracy."

AMENDED TEXT OF S. 67

S. 67 of the 1952 Act applies to the Isle of Man. The amendment also extends thereto (by virtue of s. 4 (4) para. [**32.4**], *ante*).

"**67.** (1) The Commissioners may, if they consider it necessary, require evidence to be produced to their satisfaction in support of any information required by or under this Part of this Act to be provided in respect of goods imported or exported.

(2) *Without prejudice to subsection* (1) *above, where any question as to the duties of customs chargeable on any goods, or the operation of any prohibition or restriction on importation, depends on any question as to the place from which the goods were consigned, or on any question where they or other goods are to be treated as grown, manufactured or produced, or any question as to payments made or relief from duty allowed in any country or territory, then*

(*a*) *the Commissioners may require the importer of the goods to furnish to them, in such form as they may prescribe, proof of any statement made to them as to any fact necessary to determine that question, or of the accuracy of any certificate or other document furnished in connection with the importation of the goods and relating to the matter in issue, and if such proof is not furnished to their satisfaction, the question may be determined without regard to that statement or to that certificate or document; and*

(*b*) *if in any proceedings relating to the goods or to the duty chargeable thereon the accuracy of any such certificate or document comes in question, it shall be for the person relying on it to furnish proof of its accuracy.*"

(4) At the end of section 70 there shall be added as a separate subsection (2)—

"(2) Where, in pursuance of any Community requirement or practice as to the movement of goods between countries, a seal, lock or mark is used (whether in the United Kingdom or elsewhere) to secure or identify any goods for customs purposes, and the seal, lock or mark is at any time wilfully and prematurely removed or tampered with in the United Kingdom, the person then in charge of the goods shall be liable to a penalty of £100."

AMENDED TEXT OF S. 70

S. 70 (amended by s. 4 (1) and Sched. 4A (ii) 2 (4)) relates to E.E.C. Regulation 542/69 and other secondary legislation governing Community transit. (It may be noted that Regulation 542/69 needed to be based on Art. 235 of the E.E.C. Treaty because Art. 27 does not empower the institutions of the Community to issue binding provisions in that field.) See, under sub-s. (7), AS TO THE MOVEMENT OF GOODS BETWEEN COUNTRIES.

"**70.** Where, in pursuance of any power conferred by this Act, an officer has placed any lock, mark or seal upon any goods in any ship, aircraft or vehicle, or upon any place or container in which such goods are kept, then if, without the authority of the proper officer, at any time while the ship is within the limits of any port or on passage between ports or while the aircraft or vehicle is in the United Kingdom, that lock, mark or seal is wilfully opened, altered or broken, or if, before that lock, mark or seal is lawfully removed, any of the goods are secretly conveyed away, the master of the ship or commander of the aircraft or the person in charge of the vehicle shall be liable to a penalty of one hundred pounds.

(2) *Where in pursuance of any Community requirement or practice as to the movement of goods between countries, a seal, lock or mark is used (whether in the United Kingdom or elsewhere) to secure or identify any goods for customs purposes, and the seal, lock or mark is at any time wilfully and prematurely removed or tampered with in the United Kingdom, the person then in charge of the goods shall be liable to a penalty of £100.*"

(5) In section 80 (1) (which provides for the approval of warehouses for the goods mentioned in paragraphs (*a*) to (*d*)) there shall be inserted after paragraph (*d*) as a new paragraph—

"(*e*) subject to such conditions and restrictions as aforesaid, of such other goods as the Commissioners may allow to be warehoused for exportation or for use as stores in cases where relief from or repayment of any duty of customs or other payment is conditional on their exportation or use as stores;"

and in section 88 (1) (duty chargeable on warehoused goods) there shall be inserted after the words "warehoused goods" the words "(other than those falling within section 80 (1) (*e*) of this Act)".

(6) In section 88 (4) after the word "hops" there shall be inserted the words "the proprietor of the goods may elect, if any permitted operation has been carried out on the goods in warehouse, that the amount of any duty chargeable thereon under this section, not being a duty of excise or a duty of customs other than an import duty, shall be calculated in accordance with the account last taken of the goods before any permitted operation was so carried out, but otherwise".

AMENDED TEXT OF S. 80 (1)

S. 80 enables United Kingdom traders to take advantage of the slightly less stringent Community provisions relating to warehousing of E.E.C. Regulation 69/73 ("concerning harmonization of provisions imposed by law, regulation or administrative action relating to inward processing").

"**80.** (1) The Commissioners may approve, for such period and subject to such conditions as they think fit, places of security for the deposit, keeping and securing—

(*a*) subject to such conditions and restrictions as they see fit to impose, of any goods chargeable with a duty of customs without payment of that duty;

(*b*) subject to such conditions and restrictions as aforesaid of goods for exportation or for use as stores, being goods not eligible for home use;

(*c*) of goods permitted by or under the excise Act to be warehoused without payment of any duty or excise chargeable thereon;

(*d*) of goods permitted by or under the customs of excise Acts to be warehoused on drawback;

(*e*) *subject to such conditions and restrictions as aforesaid of such other goods as the Commissioners may allow to be warehoused for exportation or for use as stores in cases where relief from or repayment of any duty of customs or other payment is conditional on their exportation or use as stores;*

and any place of security so approved is in this Act referred to as a "warehouse".

(2) The Commissioners may from time to time give directions—

(*a*) as to the goods which may or may not be deposited in any particular warehouse or class of warehouse;

(*b*) as to the part of any warehouse in which any class or description of goods may be kept or secured.

(3) If, after the approval of a warehouse, the occupier thereof makes without the previous consent of the Commissioners any alteration therein or addition thereto, he shall be liable to a penalty of two hundred pounds.

(4) The Commissioners may at any time for reasonable cause revoke or vary the terms of their approval of any warehouse under this section.

(5) Any person contravening or failing to comply with any condition imposed or direction given by the Commissioners under this section shall be liable to a penalty of one hundred pounds."

AMENDED TEXT OF S. 88 (1) AND (4)

S. 88 relates primarily to E.E.C. Directive 71/235 "concerning harmonization of provisions imposed by law, regulation or administrative action relating to normal manipulations which can be effected in customs warehouses and free zones".

"**88.** (1) Subject to the next following subsection, the duties of customs or excise and the rates thereof chargeable on warehoused goods (*other than those falling within section* 80 (1) (*e*) *of this Act*) shall be those in force with respect to goods of that class or description at the date of the removal of the goods from the warehouse.

(2) Where goods have been permitted under this Act to be removed from a warehouse without payment of duty for any purpose with the intention that they shall be rewarehoused but the goods are entered for home use before being rewarehoused, the duties of customs or excise and the rates thereof chargeable on the goods shall be those in force with respect to goods of that class or description—

(*a*) where delivery for home use is allowed under section two hundred and fifty-five of this Act on the giving of security for the duty chargeable thereon, at the date of the giving of the security; or

(*b*) in any other case, at the date of payment.

(3) Subject to the next following subsection the amount payable in respect of any duty chargeable on goods under this section shall be calculated in accordance with the account taken of the goods upon their first being warehoused.

(4) In the case of any of the following goods, that is to say, tobacco, wines spirits, figs, currants, raisins, hydrocarbon oils and hops, *the proprietor of the goods may elect, if any permitted operation has been carried out on the goods in warehouse, that the amount of any duty chargeable thereon under this section, not being a duty of excise or a duty of customs other than an import duty, shall be calculated in accordance with the account last taken of the goods before any permitted operation was so carried out, but otherwise* the amount payable in respect of any duty chargeable thereon under this section shall be calculated—

(*a*) in accordance with the account taken of those goods on their last being deposited in a warehouse; or

(*b*) where account has been taken after the carrying out of any permitted operation on the goods in warehouse since they were so last deposited, in accordance with the last account so taken

or, at the option of the proprietor of the goods, by reference to the quantity of the goods ascertained according to weight, measure or strength at the time of the delivery of the goods for home use:

Provided that this subsection shall not apply in relation to any amount payable in respect of duty under section eighty-five of this Act.

(5) Where any sum has been paid in respect of duty before the appropriate date under this section, the difference, if any, between the sum so paid and the amount properly payable shall be paid or repaid as the case may require."

See also s. 6 (5), *ante*.

(7) After section 255 there shall be inserted as a new section 255A—

"255A. Where any question as to the duties of customs chargeable on any goods depends on the use to be made of any goods or on any other matter not reasonably ascertainable from an examination of the goods, and that question is not in law conclusively determined by the production of any certificate or other document, then on the importation of those goods the Commissioners may impose such conditions as they see fit for securing that the goods will be so used or otherwise for the prevention of abuse or the protection of the revenue (including conditions requiring security for the observance of any conditions so imposed)".

AMENDED TEXT OF S. 225

S. 255 relates to s. 5 (5) (*b*).

"**255.** (1) Where it is impracticable immediately to ascertain whether any or what duty of customs is payable in respect of any imported goods which are entered for home use, whether on importation or from warehouse, the Commissioners may, if they think fit and notwithstanding any other provision of this Act, allow those goods to be delivered upon the importer giving security by deposit of money or otherwise to their satisfaction for payment of any amount unpaid which may be payable by way of duty.

(2) The Commissioners may for the purposes of the foregoing subsection treat goods as entered for home use notwithstanding that the entry does not contain all the particulars required for perfect entry if it contains as many of those particulars as are then known to the importer, and in that event the importer shall supply the remaining particulars as soon as may be to the Commissioners.

(3) Where goods are allowed to be delivered under this section, the Commissioners shall, when they have determined the amount of duty which in their opinion is payable, give to the importer a notice specifying that amount; and the amount so specified or, where any amount has been deposited under subsection (1) of this section, any difference between those amounts shall forthwith be paid or repaid as the case may require; provided that if the importer disputes the correctness of the amount so specified he may at any time within three months of the date of the said notice make such a requirement for reference to arbitration or such an application to the court as is provided for by section two hundred and sixty of this Act and that section shall have effect accordingly, so, however, that no such requirement or application shall be made until any sum falling to be paid by the importer under this subsection has been paid, and where any sum so falls to be paid no interest shall be paid under subsection (2) of that section in respect of any period before that sum is paid.

255. A. *Where any question as to the duties of customs chargeable on any goods depends on the use to be made of any goods or on any other matter not reasonably ascertainable from an examination of the goods, and that question is not in law conclusively determined by the production of any certificate or other document, then on the importation of those goods the Commissioners may impose such conditions as they see fit for securing that the goods will be so used or otherwise for the prevention of abuse or the protection of the revenue (including conditions requiring security for the observance of any conditions so imposed).*"

S. 255 of the 1952 Act applies to the Isle of Man. The amendment also extends thereto (by virtue of s. 4 (4), para. [**32.4**], *ante*).

(8) For section 258 (1) and (2) there shall be substituted, except for cases in which the value of goods falls to be determined as at a time before the entry date, a new subsection—

"(1) For the purposes of any duty of customs for the time being chargeable on any imported goods by reference to their value, whether a Community customs duty or not, the value of the goods shall be taken according to the rules applicable in the case of Community customs duties, and duty shall be paid on that value:

Provided that in relation to an importation in the course of trade within the Communities the value shall be determined on the basis of a delivery to the buyer at the port or place of importation into the United Kingdom." **[62]**

AMENDED TEXT OF S. 258

S. 258 now substitutes Community valuation law, which is all "directly applicable" (Introduction, para. [**16**] *et seq., ante*), for United Kingdom valuation law. (Sched. 6 of the Customs and Excise Act 1952 (the "valuation schedule") is consequentially repealed by s. 4 (1) and Sched. 3, Part IV "except for cases in which the value of goods falls to be determined as at a time before the entry date".) By virtue of s. 308 of the 1952 Act, s. 258 does not apply to the Isle of Man.

"**258.** (1) *For the purposes of any duty of customs for the time being chargeable on any imported goods by reference to their value, whether a Community customs duty or not, the value of the goods shall be taken according to the rules applicable in the case of Community customs duties, and duty shall be paid on that value;*

Provided that in relation to an importation in the course of trade within the

Communities the value shall be determined on the basis of a delivery to the buyer at the port or place of importation into the United Kingdom."

N.B. The above new subsection is substituted for the former sub-ss. (1) and (2) by the amendment "except for cases in which the value of goods falls to be determined as at a time before the entry date". The same exception is made in respect of the repeal, by s. 4 (1) and Sched. 3, Part IV, of Sched. 6 (the so-called "valuation Schedule") of the 1952 Act—see heading, *supra*.

"(3) The Commissioners may make regulations for the purpose of giving effect to the foregoing provisions of this section, and in particular for requiring any importer or other person concerned with the importation of goods to furnish to the Commissioners, in such form as they may require, such information as is in their opinion necessary for a proper valuation thereof, and to produce any books of account or other documents of whatever nature relating to the purchase, importation or sale of the goods by that person.

(4) If any person contravenes or fails to comply with any regulation made under this section, he shall be liable to a penalty of fifty pounds."

B: *Food*

3.—(1) In the Food and Drugs Act 1955 ("the Act of 1955"), and in the Food and Drugs (Scotland) Act 1956 ("the Act of 1956"), there shall be inserted in section 4 (1) (regulations as to composition of food etc.) after the words "protection of the public" the words "or to be called for by any Community obligation".

(2) (*a*) After section 123 of the Act of 1955 there shall be inserted as section 123A the following section:—

"(1) The Ministers may, as respects any directly applicable Community provision relating to food for which, in their opinion, it is appropriate to make provision under this Act, by regulations make such provision as they consider necessary or expedient for the purpose of securing that the Community provision is administered, executed and enforced under this Act, and may apply such of the provisions of this Act as may be specified in the regulations in relation to the Community provision with such modifications, if any, as may be so specified.

(2) For the purpose of complying with any Community obligation, or for conformity with any provision made for that purpose, the Ministers may by regulations make provision as to—

(*a*) the manner of sampling any food specified in the regulations, and the manner in which samples are to be dealt with; and

(*b*) the method to be used in analysing, testing or examining samples of any food so specified;

and regulations made by the Ministers for that purpose, or for conformity with any provision so made, may modify or exclude any provision of this Act relating to the procuring or analysis of, or dealing with, samples or to evidence of the results of an analysis or test";

and in section 124 (2) of the Act of 1955 (statutory instruments subject to annulment), in paragraph (*a*) after the words "eighty-nine" there shall be inserted the words "or section 123A".

(*b*) After section 56 of the Act of 1956 there shall be inserted as section 56A the same section as is set out in paragraph (*a*) above but with the substitution for the words "the Ministers, "their opinion" and "they consider" of the words "the Secretary of State", "his opinion" and he considers" respectively.

(*c*) In section 22 (2) of the Trade Descriptions Act 1968 (admissibility of evidence of analysis where offence is one under both that Act and food and drugs laws) after the words "123" there shall be inserted the words "or 123A" and after the word "56" there shall be inserted the words "or 56A".

(3) As from the end of the year 1975, or any earlier date which, for any provision, the Minister of Agriculture, Fisheries and Food and the Secretary of State acting

jointly may by order made by statutory instrument appoint, there shall be omitted the following provisions of the Act of 1955 or the Act of 1956, that is to say,—

(*a*) section 32 (2) of the Act of 1955 and section 17 (1) (*b*) of the Act of 1956, and the words "any separated milk, or" in section 32 (4) of the Act of 1955 and in section 17 (2) of the Act of 1956;

(*b*) section 33 of the Act of 1955, together with the words from "(being" to "Act)" in section 29 (1) (*l*) of that Act, and in section 16 of the Act of 1956 subsection (1), together with the words from "(being" to "subsection)" in subsection (2). [**63**]

OR TO BE CALLED FOR BY ANY COMMUNITY OBLIGATION

See Sched. 1, Part II, "Community obligation" Definition and Note.

S. 123

In the new s. 123A as to (1) DIRECTLY APPLICABLE and (2) COMMUNITY OBLIGATION see, in particular, Sched. 1, Part II, "Community obligation", Definition and Note; as to (1) cf. also, under s. 6 (4), SUCH PROVISION SUPPLEMENTARY.

C: *Grading etc. of Horticultural Produce*

4.—(1) Part III of the Agriculture and Horticulture Act 1964 (grading and transport of fresh horticultural produce) shall be amended as follows:—

(*a*) in section 11 (power to prescribe grades) there shall be added at the end as a new subsection (3)—

"(3) Regulations under subsection (1) above shall not apply to produce of any description for the time being subject to Community grading rules; but in relation to any such produce the Ministers may by regulations—

(*a*) make additional provision as to the form of any label required for the purpose of those rules or as to the inclusion in any such label of additional particulars (not affecting the grading of the produce);

(*b*) provide for the application, subject to any modifications specified in the regulations, of all or any of the following provisions of this Part of this Act as if the produce were regulated produce and as if the standards of quality established by those rules were prescribed grades.";

(*b*) at the end of section 22 (3) (which provides against the grading etc. of produce by agricultural marketing boards otherwise than in conformity with regulations under section 11 (1) or 21 or, in Northern Ireland, any corresponding provisions for the time being in force there) there shall be added—

"This subsection shall apply in relation to Community grading rules as it applies in relation to regulations under section 11 (1) or 21 of this Act or, as regards Northern Ireland, under any corresponding provisions.";

(*c*) in section 24 (interpretation of Part III) there shall be inserted after the definition of "authorised officer" the following definition:—

"Community grading rules" means any directly applicable Community provisions establishing standards of quality for fresh horticultural produce.

(2) In section 2 (4) of the Trade Descriptions Act 1968 (which provides that certain statutory descriptions and markings are to be deemed not to be trade descriptions) after the words "the Agriculture and Horticulture Act 1964" there shall be inserted the words "or any Community grading rules within the meaning of Part III of that Act". [**64**]

D: *Seeds and other Propagating Material*

5.—(1) In the Plant Varieties and Seeds Act 1964 there shall be made the amendments provided for by sub-paragraphs (2) to (5) below.

(2) In section 16 (1) (*c*) (preventing spread of plant disease by the sale of seeds) for the words "the sale" there shall be substituted the words "means", and after section 16 (1) there shall be inserted as subsection (1A):—

"(1A) Seeds regulations may further make provision for regulating the marketing or the importation or exportation, of seeds or any related activities (whether by reference to officially published lists of permitted varieties or otherwise),,and may in that connection include provision—

(*a*) for the registration or licensing of persons engaged in the seeds industry or related activities;

(*b*) for ensuring that seeds on any official list remain true to variety;

(*c*) for the keeping and inspection of records and the giving of information;

(*d*) for conferring rights of appeal to the Tribunal;

(*e*) for excluding, extending or modifying, in relation to or in connection with any provision of the regulations, the operation of any provision made by the following sections of this Part of this Act or of Part IV of this Act, and for the charging of fees";

and the provisions relating to offences connected with seeds regulations shall be amended as follows:—

(*a*) in section 16, for the words from "which concerns" in subsection (7) (*b*) to the end of subsection (8) there shall be substituted the words "he shall be liable on summary conviction to a fine not exceeding £400"; and

(*b*) in section 18 (2) for the words from "for an offence" in paragraph (*b*) to the end of paragraph (*c*) there shall be substituted the words "for any other offence"; and

(*c*) in section 25 (7) for paragraphs (*a*) and (*b*) there shall be substituted the words "to a fine not exceeding one hundred pounds".

(3) At the end of section 16 there shall be added a subsection (8)—

"(8) The Ministers acting jointly may make seeds regulations for the whole of Great Britain".

(4) In section 29 (which extends Part II to seed potatoes) after the words "seed potatoes", in both places, there shall be inserted the words "to any other vegetative propagating material and to silvicultural planting material", and at the end of that section there shall be added as subsections (2) and (3)—

(2) The Forestry Commissioners may establish and maintain an official seed testing station for silvicultural propagating and planting material, and seeds regulations may confer on those Commissioners any functions the regulations may confer on a Minister, and the Commissioners may charge or authorise the charging of fees for services given at any such station or in connection with any such functions; and accordingly

(*a*) references in this Part of this Act to an authorised officer shall include an officer of those Commissioners; and

(*b*) in section 25 above the references in subsections (3), (4) and (6) to a person duly authorised by the Minister shall include a person duly authorised by the Commissioners.

Any expenses incurred or fees received by the Commissioners by virtue of this subsection shall be paid out of or into the Forestry Fund.

(3) In relation to matters concerning silvicultural propagating or planting material or concerning the Forestry Commissioners, 'the Minister' shall in this Part of this Act mean, in relation to Wales and Monmouthshire, the Secretary

of State, and the reference in section 16 (8) to the Ministers shall be construed accordingly."

Accordingly in section 30 (1) in the definition of "official testing station" there shall be omitted the words "by the Minister or Ministers", and in section 38 (1) in the definition of "the Minister" after the word "means" there shall be inserted the words "(subject to section 29 (3))".

(5) In section 10 (1) for the name "Plant Variety Rights Tribunal" there shall be substituted the name "Plant Varieties and Seeds Tribunal", and in paragraph 5 (1) of Schedule 4 there shall be added at the end of paragraph (*b*) (which sets up, to furnish members of the Tribunal, a panel of persons with specialised knowledge) the words "or of the seeds industry".

(6) In Part III of Schedule 1 to the House of Commons Disqualification Act 1957, as amended by the Plant Varieties and Seeds Act 1964 (both for the Parliament of the United Kingdom and for the Parliament of Northern Ireland), and in Schedule 1 to the Tribunals and Inquiries Act 1971, for the name 'Plant Variety Rights Tribunal' there shall be substituted in each place the name 'Plant Varieties and Seeds Tribunal'." **[65]**

E: *Fertilisers and Feeding Stuffs*

6. After section 74 of the Agriculture Act 1970 there shall be inserted as a new section 74A—

"74A.—(1) Regulations under this Part of this Act, with a view to controlling in the public interest the composition or content of fertilisers and of material intended for the feeding of animals, may make provision—

(*a*) prohibiting or restricting, by reference to its composition or content, the importation into and exportation from the United Kingdom, the sale or possession with a view to sale, or the use, of any prescribed material;

(*b*) regulating the marking, labelling and packaging of prescribed material and the marks to be applied to any container or vehicle in which any prescribed material is enclosed or conveyed.

(2) Regulations made under subsection (1) above with respect to any material may include provision excluding or modifying the operation in relation to that material of any other provision of this Part of this Act; but, subject to any provision so made, references in this Part of this Act to feeding stuffs shall apply to all material which is intended for the feeding of animals and with respect to which regulations are for the time being in force under that subsection.

(3) Any person who contravenes any prohibition or restriction imposed by regulations under subsection (1) above, or fails to comply with any other provision of the regulations, shall be liable on summary conviction to a fine not exceeding £400 or, on a second or subsequent conviction, to a fine not exceeding £400 or to imprisonment for a term not exceeding three months, or to both.

(4) With a view to implementing or supplementing any Community instrument relating to fertilisers or to material intended for the feeding of animals, regulations may provide for the application, in relation to any material specified in the regulations, of all or any of the provisions of this Part of this Act, subject to any modifications which may be so specified." **[66]**

F: *Animal Health*

7.—(1) In the Diseases of Animals Act 1950 there shall be made, with effect from the entry date, the amendments provided for by the following sub-paragraphs.

(2) At the end of section 25 (imported animals to be slaughtered on landing) there shall be added—

"other than animals of any such description as may be prescribed by order of the Minister which are brought from a member State and in relation to which any conditions so prescribed are satisfied; but where Part I (slaughter) of the First Schedule to this Act is under this section not to apply to animals so brought, the Minister may by order provide that Part II (quarantine) and Part III (ancillary provisions) shall apply, with or without modification.

An order under this section shall be subject to annulment in pursuance of a resolution of either House of Parliament."

(3) After section 36 there shall be inserted a new section 36A—

"36A. The Minister may by order make provision in the interests of animal health or of human health, for regulating the exportation from Great Britain to a member State of animals or poultry or carcases thereof, and in particular for prohibiting exportation without such certificate or licence as may be prescribed by the order, and as to the circumstances in which and conditions on which a certificate or licence may be obtained".

(4) In section 49 (1) (*a*) (control of import of poultry) after the word "poultry", in the first two places where it occurs, there shall be inserted the words "or carcases of poultry".

(5) At the end of section 19 (6) (power to withhold or reduce compensation for slaughter of animal imported when diseased) there shall be added the words "or, before or while being brought from a member State, exposed to infection of disease". **[67]**

G: *Plant Health*

8.—(1) In the Plant Health Act 1967 there shall be made, with effect from the entry date, the amendments provided for by the following sub-paragraphs.

(2) In section 1 (1) (by which the Act has effect for the control in Great Britain of plant pests and diseases) the words "in Great Britain" shall be omitted; and—

(*a*) in section 2 (1) and section 3 (1) (orders for control of pests) after the words "thinks expedient" there shall be inserted the words "or called for by any Community obligation";

(*b*) at the end of section 3 (1), after the words "preventing the spread of pests in Great Britain", there shall be added the words "or the conveyance of pests by articles exported from Great Britain";

(*c*) in section 3 (5) (which extends the time limit for summary prosecutions of certain offences) there shall be omitted the words "where the offence is one in connection with the movement, sale, consignment or planting of potatoes".

(3) In section 3 (2) (*a*) (which provides for the removal or destruction of infected crops etc.) there shall be inserted after the word "removal" the word "treatment" and after the words "any seed, plant or part thereof" the words "or any container, wrapping or other article", and in section 3 (2) (*b*) (which provides for entry on land for those and other purposes) there shall be inserted after the word "removal" the word "treatment" and after the word "land" the words "or elsewhere"; and the words "or elsewhere" shall also be inserted after the word "land" in section 4 (1)(*b*) (which also relates to entry).

(4) At the end of section 6 (1) there shall be added the words "or, in the case of an order prohibiting or regulating the landing in or exportation from Great Britain of any articles, shall be subject to annulment in pursuance of a resolution of either House of Parliament". **[68]**

H: *Road Vehicles (Driving under Age, and Drivers' Hours)*

9.—(1) In section 4 (4) of the Road Traffic Act 1972 (offence of driving below the permitted age) there shall be added at the end the words "and this subsection shall apply to a contravention in Great Britain of any directly applicable Community provision relating to the driving of road vehicles on international journeys, being a provision as to the minimum age for driving a vehicle of any description, as it applies to a contravention of the provisions of this section".

(2) In Part VI of the Transport Act 1968, in section 103 (1), after the definition of "employer" there shall be inserted the words " 'the international rules' means any directly applicable Community provision relating to the driving of road vehicles on international journeys"; and—

(*a*) after section 96 (11) there shall be inserted as subsection (11A)—

"(11A) Where, in the case of a driver or member of the crew of a motor vehicle, there is in Great Britain a contravention of any requirement of the international rules as to periods of driving, or distance driven, or periods on or off duty, then the offender and any other person (being the offender's employer or a person to whose orders the offender was subject) who caused or permitted the contravention shall be liable on summary conviction to a fine not exceeding £200";

and in section 98 (4) (failure to comply with regulations as to keeping of records etc.) after the words "regulations made under this section" their shall be inserted the words "or any requirement as to books or records of the international rules", in section 98 (5) after the words "of regulations under this section" there shall be inserted the words "or of the international rules", and in section 99 (5) (falsification of records) after the words "regulations under section 98 thereof" there shall be inserted the words "or the international rules";

(*b*) in section 99 (1) (power of enforcement officer to inspect records and other documents) there shall be inserted after paragraph (*c*)—

"(*d*) any corresponding book, register or document required by the international rules or which the officer may reasonably require to inspect for the purpose of ascertaining whether the requirements of the international rules have been complied with";

and in section 99 (3) after the words "subsection (1) (*a*)" there shall be inserted "or (*d*)";

(*c*) in section 98 (2) (power to make provision supplementary and incidental to the provision made under section 98 (1) as to the keeping of books and records) there shall be inserted after the words "supplementary and incidental provisions" the words "including provisions supplementary and incidental to the requirements of the international rules as to books and records", and after the words "for the purpose of the regulations" in paragraph (*a*) the words "or of the international rules".

(3) At the end of section 95 (1) of the Transport Act 1968 there shall be added the words—

"but the Secretary of State may by regulations make such provision supplemental or incidental to, or by way of adaptation of, this Part of this Act as is in his opinion called for to take account, in relation to journeys and work to which the international rules apply, of the operation of those rules and to ensure compatibility of operation between section 96 (1) to (9) as they apply to other journeys and work and the international rules; and regulations made under this subsection—

(*a*) may in particular make exceptions from the operation of section 96 (1) to (6), and include provision as to the circumstances in which a period of driving or duty to which the international rules apply is to be included or excluded in reckoning any period for purposes of section 96 (1) to (6); and

(*b*) may contain such transitional and supplementary provisions as the Secretary of State thinks necessary or expedient;

and a reference to the international rules shall be deemed to be included in any reference to this Part of this Act in sections 35 (2) (*b*), 62 (4) (*b*) and 64 (2) (*c*) of this Act and in paragraph 2 (5) of Schedule 9 thereto."

(4) In the following provisions as amended by the Transport Act 1968 (which, as so amended, allow records kept under Part VI of that Act to be inspected), that is

to say, in section 11 (1) (*a*) of the Road Haulage Wages Act 1938 and in section 19 (3) (*b*) of the Wages Councils Act 1959, after the words "Part VI of the Transport Act 1968" there shall be inserted the words "or of the international rules within the meaning of the said Part VI"; and in Schedule 2 to the Road Traffic (Foreign Vehicles) Act 1972, in the entry relating to sections 96 to 98 of the Transport Act 1968 and regulations and orders thereunder, there shall be added at the end of the words in the first column the words "and the international rules within the meaning of Part VI of that Act". **[69]**

DIRECTLY APPLICABLE COMMUNITY PROVISION

See Introduction, para. [**16**], *ante*, and Sched. 1, Part II, "Community obligation", Definition and Note.

I: *Road Transport* (*International Passenger Services*)

10. In section 160 (1) of the Road Traffic Act 1960 (regulations with respect to licensing of public service vehicles), in paragraph (*k*) after the word "vehicles" there shall be inserted the words "registered elsewhere than in Great Britain or" and the following shall be added at the end of the subsection:—

"(*l*) exempting vehicles from the requirement of a road service licence when used under an authorisation granted in pursuance of any directly applicable Community provision regulating the provision of international passenger-carrying road transport services

(*m*) requiring documents of any prescribed description relevant to the administration or enforcement of any such Community provision to be kept and produced on demand for the inspection of a prescribed person;

(*n*) prescribing persons to act as authorised inspection officers for the purposes of any such Community provision;"

and at the end of section 239 of that Act (penalty for contravention of regulations) there shall be inserted the words "and where any such directly applicable Community provision as is referred to in section 160 (1) (*l*) of this Act requires the keeping or production of any document, any person who contravenes that requirement shall be guilty of an offence under this section." **[70]**

SECTION 160 (1)

In (*l*) and at the end of s. 239, addition, DIRECTLY APPLICABLE COMMUNITY PROVISION, see Introduction, paras. [**16**] *et seq.*, and Sched. 1, Part II, "Community obligation", Definition and Note.

The addition at the end of s. 239 of the Road Traffic Act 1960 creates a new offence.

DIVISION III

SELECTED ORDERS

The Intervention Board for Agricultural Produce Order 1972

(S.I. 1972 No. 1578)

Whereas section 6 (1) of the European Communities Act 1972 provides that there shall be a Board in charge of a government department, by the name of the Intervention Board for Agricultural Produce, and that the Board (in addition to any other functions that may be entrusted to it) shall be charged, subject to the direction and control of the Minister of Agriculture, Fisheries and Food, the Secretary of State for Wales and the Secretaries of State respectively concerned with agriculture in Scotland and Northern Ireland, acting jointly, with such functions as those Ministers (who are hereinafter referred to as the Ministers) may from time to time determine in connection with the carrying out of the obligations of the United Kingdom under the common agricultural policy of the European Economic Community:

And Whereas section 6 (2) of the said Act enables Her Majesty by Order in Council to make further provision as to the constitution and membership of the Board, and the remuneration (including pensions) of members of the Board or any committee thereof, and for regulating or facilitating the discharge of the Board's functions, including provision for the Board to arrange for its functions to be performed by other bodies on its behalf and any such provision as was made by Schedule 1 to the Ministers of the Crown Act 1964 in relation to a Minister to whom that Schedule applied:

Now, therefore, Her Majesty, in exercise of the powers conferred upon Her by section 6 (2) of the European Communities Act 1972, is pleased, by and with the advice of Her Privy Council, to order, and it is hereby ordered, as follows:—

1.—(1) This Order may be cited as the Intervention Board for Agricultural Produce Order 1972.

(2) The Interpretation Act 1889 shall apply for the interpretation of this Order as it applies for the interpretation of an Act of Parliament.

(3) This Order shall come into operation on 22nd November 1972. **[71]**

2. The provisions of the Schedule to this Order shall have effect with respect to the Intervention Board for Agricultural Produce and its committees and the other matters there mentioned. **[72]**

SCHEDULE

Members, Committees and Staff

1.—(1) The Intervention Board for Agricultural Produce shall consist of such number of members, appointed by the Ministers, as the Ministers may from time to time determine.

(2) The Ministers may appoint one member of the Board to be chairman, and another to be deputy chairman.

(3) Subject to the following sub-paragraphs and to paragraph 2 below, a member of the Board and the chairman and deputy chairman shall each hold and vacate office as such in accordance with the terms of his appointment.

(4) If the chairman or deputy chairman ceases to be a member of the Board, he shall also cease to be chairman or deputy chairman.

(5) A member of the Board may at any time, by notice in writing addressed to the Ministers or any of them, resign his membership, and the chairman or deputy chairman may, by the like notice, resign his office as such.

2.—(1) Where a member of the Board has been appointed for a fixed term, and the Ministers are satisfied—

(*a*) that he has become bankrupt or made an arrangement with his creditors; or

(*b*) that he is incapacitated by physical or mental illness; or

(*c*) that he is otherwise unable or unfit to discharge the functions of a member;

the Ministers may declare his office as a member of the Board to be vacant, and shall notify the fact in such manner as the Ministers think fit; and thereupon the office shall become vacant.

(2) In the application of this paragraph to Scotland, for the references in head (*a*) of sub-paragraph (1) to a member's having become bankrupt and to a member's having made an arrangement with his creditors there shall be substituted respectively references to sequestration of a member's estate having been awarded and to a member's having made a trust deed for behoof of his creditors or a composition contract.

3.—(1) The Ministers may after consultation with the Board by direction establish one or more committees of the Board for the purpose of performing any of the functions of the Board specified in the direction or of advising the Board on any matters so specified.

(2) Any such committee shall consist of such number of members, appointed by the Ministers from among the members of the Board or otherwise, as the Ministers may from time to time determine.

(3) In relation to any such committee sub-paragraphs (2) to (5) of paragraph 1 above and paragraph 2 above shall apply as they apply in relation to the Board.

4.—(1) The Board shall pay to the members of the Board or any committee thereof such salaries or fees and allowances as may be determined by the Ministers with the approval of the Minister for the Civil Service.

(2) In the case of any such person who is or has been a member of the Board or any committee thereof as may be determined by the Ministers with the approval of the Minister for the Civil Service, the Board shall pay such pension, allowance or gratuity to or in respect of him, or make such payments towards the provision of such a pension, allowance or gratuity, as may be so determined.

(3) Where a person ceases to be a member of the Board or any committee thereof otherwise than on the expiry of his term of office and it appears to the Ministers that there are special circumstances which make it right for that person to receive compensation, the Ministers may, with the approval of the Minister for the Civil Service, direct the Board to make to that person a payment of such amount as the Ministers may with that approval determine.

(4) As soon as practicable after the making of any determination under sub-paragraph (2) or (3) above, the Ministers shall lay a statement thereof before each House of Parliament.

5.—(1) The Ministers shall appoint a person to be Chief Executive of the Board, and the Board may appoint such other officers and servants as it may with the approval of the Ministers and the Minister for the Civil Service determine.

(2) The Chief Executive may be a member of the Board, but shall not also be chairman nor be paid as a member of the Board.

PROCEEDINGS

6.—(1) In the event of an equality of votes at any meeting of the Board or a committee thereof, the person who is chairman at that meeting shall have a second or casting vote.

(2) A member of the Board or of a committee thereof shall, if he is in any way directly or indirectly interested in a contract made or proposed to be made by the Board, disclose the nature of his interest at a meeting of the Board or committee as soon as possible after the relevant circumstances have come to his knowledge; and any disclosure made under this sub-paragraph shall be recorded in the minutes of the Board or committee, and the member shall not take part after the disclosure in any deliberation or decision of the Board or committee with respect to the contract (but may, nevertheless, be taken into account for the purpose of constituting a quorum of the Board or committee).

(3) Subject to sub-paragraphs (1) and (2) above, the Board may determine its own quorum and procedure and the quorum and procedure of any committee of the Board.

EXECUTION AND PROOF OF DOCUMENTS

7.—(1) The application of the seal of the Board shall be authenticated by the signature of a member of the Board, or of the Chief Executive or some person authorised by the Board to act on behalf of the Chief Executive.

(2) The seal of the Board shall be officially and judicially noticed and every document purporting to be an instrument made or issued by the Board and to be sealed with the seal of the Board authenticated as mentioned above, or signed by the Chief Executive or a person authorised by the Board to act on behalf of the Chief Executive, shall be received in evidence and be deemed to be such an instrument without further proof, unless the contrary is shown.

(3) The Documentary Evidence Act 1868, as amended by the Documentary Evidence Act 1882, shall apply to the Board as if the Board were included in the first column of the Schedule to the Documentary Evidence Act 1868, and any member of the Board or the Chief Executive or a person authorised by the Board to act on behalf of the Chief Executive were mentioned in the second column of the Schedule, and as if the regulations referred to in those Acts included any documents issued by the Board.

SUPPLEMENTARY

8. The Board may with the approval of the Ministers arrange for the performance of any of its functions by another body created by a statutory provision and concerned with agriculture or agricultural produce.

The European Communities (Enforcement of Community Judgments) Order 1972

(S.I. 1972 No. 1590)

Her Majesty, in exercise of the powers conferred on Her by section 2 (2) of the European Communities Act 1972, is pleased, by and with the advice of Her Privy Council, to order, and it is hereby ordered, as follows:—

Citation and commencement

1. This Order may be cited as the European Communities (Enforcement of Community Judgments) Order 1972 and shall come into operation on the date on which the United Kingdom becomes a member of the European Communities. **[73]**

Interpretation

2.—(1) In this Order—

"Community judgment" means any decision, judgment or order which is enforceable under or in accordance with Article 187 or 192 of the E.E.C. Treaty, Article 18, 159 or 164 of the Euratom Treaty or Article 44 or 92 of the E.C.S.C. Treaty;

"Euratom inspection order" means an order made by or in the exercise of the functions of the President of the European Court or by the Commission of the European Communities under Article 81 of the Euratom Treaty;

"order for enforcement" means an order by or under the authority of the Secretary of State that the Community judgment to which it is appended is to be registered for enforcement in the United Kingdom; and

"the High Court" means in England and in Northern Ireland the High Court and in Scotland the Court of Session.

(2) The Interpretation Act 1889 shall apply to the interpretation of this Order as it applies to the interpretation of an Act of Parliament. **[74]**

Registration of Community judgments and orders

3.—(1) The High Court shall, upon application duly made for the purpose by the person entitled to enforce it, forthwith register any Community judgment to which the Secretary of State has appended an order for enforcement or any Euratom inspection order.

(2) Where a sum of money is payable under a Community judgment which is to be registered, the judgment shall be registered as if it were a judgment for such sum in the currency of the United Kingdom as, on the basis of the rate of exchange prevailing at the date when the Community judgment was originally given, is equivalent to the sum so payable.

(3) Rules of court shall be made requiring notice to be given of the registration of a Community judgment or Euratom inspection order to the persons against whom the judgment was given or the order was made.

(4) Where it appears that a Community judgment under which a sum of money is payable has been partly satisfied at the date of the application for its registration, the judgment shall be registered only in respect of the balance remaining payable at that date.

(5) Where, after the date of registration of a Community judgment under which a sum of money is payable, it is shown that at that date the judgment had been partly or wholly satisfied, the registration shall be varied or cancelled accordingly with effect from that date. [**75**]

Effect of registration of Community judgment

4. A Community judgment registered in accordance with Article 3 shall, for all purposes of execution, be of the same force and effect, and proceedings may be taken on the judgment, and any sum payable under the judgment shall carry interest, as if the judgment had been a judgment or order given or made by the High Court on the date of registration. [**76**]

Suspension of enforcement of Community judgments

5. An order of the European Court that enforcement of a registered Community judgment be suspended shall, on production to the High Court, be registered forthwith and shall be of the same effect as if the order had been an order made by the High Court on the date of its registration staying or sisting the execution of the judgment for the same period and on the same conditions as are stated in the order of the European Court; and no steps to enforce the judgment shall thereafter be taken while such an order remains in force. [**77**]

Effect of registration of Euratom inspection order

6. Upon registration of a Euratom inspection order in accordance with Article 3, the High Court may make such order as it thinks fit against any person for the purpose of ensuring that effect is given to the Euratom inspection order. [**78**]

INDEX

ACCESSION TREATY. *See* TREATY OF ACCESSION
AGRICULTURE,
  amendment of law, 2, 60
    commencement, 32.1
  arrangements for guaranteed prices or assured markets, 34, 34.9, 34.14, 34.15
  Channel Islands, application of Community provisions to, 28.1
  commencement of Community policy, 34.1
  cost of support of, 30.8
  Gibraltar, position of, in relation to, 28.2
  goods exported from U.K., 34, 34.11, 34.12, 34.13
  goods imported into U.K., 34, 34.14
  implementation of Community agricultural policy, 34, 34.1–34.15
  Intervention Board for Agricultural Produce, 34, 34.1, 34.2, 34.3, 34.6, 34.9, 34.10, 71
  Isle of Man, application of Community provisions to, 28.1
  levies, 30.9, 34, 34.1, 34.11, 34.12, 34.13, 34.14, 34.15
    commencement, 34.12
  Northern Ireland, implementation in, 34.2
  phased substitution of Community law, 31.7, 32.1, 34.1
ANIMAL HEALTH, 67
APPLICABILITY,
  Community law, of, without intervention of Parliament, 30

BALANCE OF PAYMENTS,
  support between member states, 30.7

CHANNEL ISLANDS,
  application to, of—
    Community agricultural provisions, 28.1
    Community customs regime, 28.1
CHANNEL ISLANDS—*continued*
  application to, of—*continued*
    E.C.S.C. Treaty, 28.1
    E.E.C. Treaty, 28.1
    Euratom Treaty, 28.1
  implementation of Treaties in, 28.2, 29, 30, 30.11, 32, 32.4
  inclusion of, in European Communities, 1, 28, 28.1, 28.2
CINEMATOGRAPH FILMS,
  amendment of law, 2, 36
  Community—
    equated with British, 36, 36.1–36.4
    registered under Films Act 1960 and 1970 36, 36.1
  Council, 36, 36.4
  definition of Community film, 36, 36.2
  substitution of Community law, 31.7
COAL,
  amendment of law, 32.1, 60
  customs duties, 33.1, 33.7
  substitution of Community law, 32.1
COAL AND STEEL COMMUNITY. *See further* EUROPEAN COAL AND STEEL COMMUNITY.
  definition of, 48
COMMUNITIES. *See also* EURATOM; EUROPEAN COAL AND STEEL COMMUNITY; EUROPEAN ECONOMIC COMMUNITY
  autonomous legal order, each an, 11–15
  definition of, 29
  furnishing information to, extension of U.K. law to cover its Community obligations, 31.7
  implementation of obligations of, 30, 3.10
  objects of, 30.7
  payments to, 29, 30, 30.7
COMMUNITY COMMITTEE, 39.7, 50
COMMUNITY CUSTOMS DUTY,
  definition of, 49
COMMUNITY FILM,
  definition of, 36, 36.2

All references are to paragraph numbers

COMMUNITY INSTITUTION,
definition of, 39, 39.6, 50, 51
document in custody of, as evidence, 31, 31.4, 31.5
COMMUNITY INSTRUMENTS,
agriculture, concerned with, 34.1
decisions on and proof of, 29, 31
definition of, 50, 51
evidence, as, 31, 31.4, 31.5, 31.6
films, for, 36, 36.3
question as to meaning or effect of, treated as question of law, 31, 31.1
COMMUNITY JUDGMENTS,
enforcement of, 78
COMMUNITY LAW. *See also* EUROPEAN COURT; TREATIES
application of, to U.K., 1–27, 29, 31, 31.1–31.7
application of, to U.K., commencment, 31.1
directly applicable, 7, 9, 10, 16–24, 26, 30.1, 30.2, 30.9, 34, 34.13, 35, 35.2, 35.3, 38, 38.2–38.5, 38.7–38.9
each Community an autonomous legal order, 11–15
enforcement of, 28, 28.1, 28.2, 29, 30, 30.2, 30.3, 38, 38.2
evidence of, provisions regarding, 31, 31.1, 31.4, 31.5
interpretation of, 23–27
question of law, not fact, to be treated as, 31, 31.1
statutes, construction of, in U.K., 23
substitution for, or incorporation in, U.K. law, 31.7, 32, 32.1
supremacy of, 15, 30.10, 38.1
treaties which are the source of, 29
U.K. application of, in relation to—
agriculture, 34, 34.1–34.15
cinematograph films, 31.7, 36, 36.1–36.4
companies, 31.7, 37, 37.1–37.10
customs duties, 30.7, 31.7, 32.1, 33, 33.1–33.24
restrictive trade practices, 31.7, 38, 38.1–38.10
sugar, 31.7, 32.1, 35, 35.1–35.4
COMMUNITY OBLIGATIONS,
agriculture, in relation to, 34, 34.5, 34.14, 34.15
cinematograph films, for, 36.1
companies, for, 37.1
customs duties, for, compliance with, 33, 33.16, 33.19
definition of, 52, 53
furnishing of information to the Communities, for, 37.1, 40, 40.1
implementation of, in U.K., 9, 10, 29.1, 30, 30.3, 30.6, 30.7, 30.11, 31.7, 32, 32.1
payments, U.K. to make, 30, 30.7
prosecute, to, for Community offences, 37.1, 39, 39.1
restrictive trade practices, for, 38, 38.2, 38.4, 38.10
COMMUNITY OBLIGATIONS—*continued*
sugar, for, 35.2
COMMUNITY OFFENCES,
communication of classified Euratom information, 39, 39.1, 39.5–39.7
extension of U.K. law to cover its Community obligations, 2, 31.7, 39, 39.1–39.7
perjury, 39, 39.1–39.5
COMMUNITY TREATIES. *See further under* TREATIES
definition of, 29
COMPANY LAW,
amendment of U.K., to conform with Community, 2, 37, 37.1
company documents, publication of, in the Gazette, 37, 37.4
Northern Ireland, implementation of Community law in, 37.9
notification of—
alteration of company's memorandum or articles or association, 37, 37.5
appointment of liquidator, 37, 37.5
change among company's directors, 37, 37.5
change in situation of company's registered office, 37, 37.5
winding-up order, 37, 37.5
pre-incorporation contracts, provision in respect of, 37, 37.3
registration of alteration in a company's memorandum or articles—
before entry date, 37, 37.5, 37.6
on or after entry date, 37, 37.5
service of documents on an unregistered company, 37, 37.8, 37.9
substitution of Community law, 31.7, 37, 37.1–37.10
commencement of, 37, 37.10
ultra vires doctrine, modification of, 37, 37.2
COURT OF JUSTICE OF THE EUROPEAN COMMUNITIES. *See* EUROPEAN COURT
CUSTOMS DUTIES,
amendment of law, 2, 32.1, 33.14, 60, 61, 62
Channel Islands, arrangements for, 28.1
community, 30.9, 33, 33.1–33.6, 33.10, 49
continuance of existing law, 33, 33.13
deferment of payment, 30.8
evidence of origin of goods, on exportation, Community requirement for, 33
Gibraltar, not included, 28.2
implementation of Community obligations in relation to, 33, 33.16–33.21
Import Duties Act 1958, powers and provisions of, 33, 33.10, 33.11, 33.12, 33.16, 33.17

All references are to paragraph numbers

CUSTOMS DUTIES—*continued*
import duties, substitution of Community, 33, 33.16, 33.17
Isle of Man, arrangements for, 28.1
levied, or not levied, in derogation of Community customs arrangements, 33, 33.3, 33.8, 33.9
Northern Ireland, application to, 33.24
phased replacement of existing, 30.7, 31.7, 32.1, 33, 33.1–33.24
commencement, 32.1, 33, 33.1, 33.2, 33.4, 33.5
progressive abolition of, on imports between the Community, 33, 33.1
progressive adjustment to Community tariffs, 33. 33.1, 33.16
reciprocal arrangements made between member states, 33, 33.22

DEFINITIONS,
Coal and Steel Community, 48
Communities, 29
Community customs duty, 49
Community film, 36, 36.2
Community institution, 39, 39.6, 50, 51
Community instrument, 50, 51
Community obligation, 52, 53
Community Treaties, 29
Economic Community, 48
E.C.S.C. Treaty, 41
E.E.C. Treaty, 42
enforceable Community right, 52, 53
entry date, 54
Euratom, 48
Euratom Treaty, 43
European Coal and Steel Community, 48
European Court, 55
member, in expression "member state" 56
Merger Treaty, 45
pre-accession treaties, 41–47
treaties, 29
treaty, for purposes of s. 1 (2), (3), 29, 29.4
Treaty of Luxembourg, 46

ECONOMIC COMMUNITY. *See further under* EUROPEAN ECONOMIC COMMUNITY
definition of, 48
E.C.S.C. TREATY,
application of—
Channel Islands, to, 28.1
Isle of Man, to, 28.1
definition of, 41
European Court, powers given to, in, 31.1
legal techniques, novelty of, 3–8
Merger Treaty, provisions for authorisation of, 38.9
E.E.C. TREATY,
application of—
Channel Islands, to, 28.1
Isle of Man, to, 28.1
definition of, 42

E.E.C. TREATY—*continued*
European Court, powers given to, in, 31.1
legal techniques, novelty of, 3–8
ENACTMENTS,
construction of, 30.10
definition of, 30.2
present and future, 30, 30.10
ENFORCEABLE COMMUNITY RIGHT, 30.1, 30.3
definition of, 52, 53
ENTRY DATE,
definition of, 54
EURATOM. *See also* COMMUNITIES
accession of U.K. to, 29
classified information, communication of, 39, 39.1, 39.5–39.7
definition of, 48
European Court, powers given to, in, 31.1
inclusion in Communities, 29
EURATOM TREATY,
application of—
Isle of Man, to, 28.1
Channel Islands, to, 28.1
definition of, 43
legal techniques, novelty of, 3–8
EUROPEAN ATOMIC ENERGY COMMUNITY. *See* EURATOM
EUROPEAN COAL AND STEEL COMMUNITY. *See also* COMMUNITIES
accession of U.K. to, decision relating to, 29
definition of, 48
inclusion in Communities, 29
Treaty. *See* E.C.S.C. TREATY
unified tariff, 33.7
U.K. investment in, 30.7
EUROPEAN COURT. *See also* COMMUNITY LAW
Community Regulations, clarification of, by, 21, 22
decisions of, 19, 20, 29, 31, 31.3
definition of, 55
evidence in, 31, 31.4, 31.5, 31.6
independence of, 13
interpretation of Treaties by, 31, 31.2
judicial notice of Treaties to be taken by, 29, 31, 31.4
perjury in proceedings before, 39, 39.1–39.5
powers of, 31, 31.1
principles laid down by, 18, 29, 31, 31.2
EUROPEAN ECONOMIC COMMUNITY. *See also* COMMUNITIES
accession of U.K. to, 29
inclusion in Communities, 29
Treaty. *See* E.E.C. TREATY
EUROPEAN INVESTMENT BANK, contributions to, 29, 30, 30.7
EVIDENCE,
Community law, in, 31, 31.1, 31.4, 31.5, 31.6
Scottish, in Community law, 31, 31.6

All references are to paragraph numbers

FERTILISERS AND FEEDING STUFFS, 66
FINANCE,
amendment of law, 60
commencement, 32.1
substitution of Community Law, 32.1
FOOD, 63
FREEDOM OF ESTABLISHMENT,
implementation of, 30.3

GIBRALTAR,
agriculture, position in relation to, 28.2
customs territory, not included in, 28.2
implementation of Treaties in, 28.2, 29, 30, 30.11
import liberalisation system, position in relation to, 28.2
inclusion of, in European Communities, 1, 28, 28.2
value added tax, position in relation to, 28.2

HORTICULTURAL PRODUCE, 64

IMPORT LIBERALISATION SYSTEM,
Gibraltar, position of, in relation to, 28.2
INFORMATION,
furnishing of, to Communities, extension of U.K. law, 2, 37.1, 40, 40.1
INTERNATIONAL LAW,
position of U.K. in relation to, 29.3
INTERNATIONAL ORGANISATIONS,
amendment of law, 60
commencement, 32.1
substitution of Community law, 32.1
INTERVENTION BOARD FOR AGRICULTURAL PRODUCE, 34, 34.1–34.3, 34.6, 34.9, 34.10, 71
IRON AND STEEL,
customs duties, 33.7
amendment of law, 60
commencement, 32.1
substitution of Community Law, 32.1
ISLE OF MAN,
application to, of—
Community agricultural provisions, 28.1
Community customs regime, 28.1
E.C.S.C. Treaty, 28.1
E.E.C. Treaty, 28.1
Euratom Treaty, 28.1
implementation of Treaties, in, 28.2, 29, 30, 30.11, 32, 32.4
inclusion of, in European Communities, 1, 28, 28.1, 28.2

LEGAL ORDER,
each Community an autonomous, 11–15
United Kingdom and Communities, dichotomy between, 28
LEGAL PROCEEDINGS,
documentary evidence in, 31, 31.4–31.6

MEDICAL TREATMENT,
payments for, 30.8
MEMBER,
definition of, in expression "member State", 56
MERGER TREATY, 38.9, 45
MUNICIPAL COURTS,
application of community law by, 30.2

NORTHERN IRELAND,
agricultural policy, implementation of, 34.2
Community films in, 35.1
Community obligation to punish for perjury, 39
customs and excise provisions, application of, 33.24
implementation of Treaties in, 29, 30, 30.10, 32, 32.3
Parliament of, applying Community law, 30, 32, 32.3
subordinate legislation, provisions as to, 59
sugar, arrangements for, implementation of, 35, 35.4

PARLIAMENT,
applying Community agricultural policy, 34, 34.1, 34.2, 34.14
applying Community customs duties, 33, 33.1–33.24
applying Community law, 5, 30, 31.7, 32, 32.1, 32.2
applying provisions as to sugar, 35, 35.1
PAYMENTS,
United Kingdom, by, to the Communities, 29, 30, 30.7, 30.8
PLANT HEALTH, 68
POWERS,
exercise of, 30, 30.10
PRE-ACCESSION TREATIES, 29, 29.1, 29.2, 41–47

REGULATIONS, COMMUNITY,
adaptation of, by member State, 30.7
application of, 21, 22, 23, 30.2
implementation of, 31.7
RESTRICTIVE TRADE PRACTICES,
amendment of law, 2. 38
compatible operation of U.K. law and Community law, 31.7, 38, 38.1–38.10
Registrar, role of, 38, 38.4, 38.7, 38.10
Restrictive Practices Court, 38, 38.1, 38.4, 38.5, 38.6
supremacy of Community law, 38.1
void agreement, 38, 38.3, 38.4
ROAD TRANSPORT, 70
ROAD VEHICLES, 69

SCOTLAND,
Community obligation to punish for perjury, 39
documentary evidence in legal proceedings in, 31, 31.6

All references are to paragraph numbers

SEEDS,
amendment of law, 60, 65
commencement, 32.1
substitution of Community Law, 32.1
SOCIAL SECURITY,
payments for, 30.8
SOVEREIGNTY, 5, 13
SUBORDINATE LEGISLATION,
common agricultural policy, for implementing, 34, 34.5, 34.8, 34.13–34.15
Community customs duties, for applying, 33, 33.18, 33.20
designated Ministry or department, 30, 30.6
enforcement of Community judgments, for, 72
implementing Treaties, 29, 30, 30.10
commencement, 30.4, 30.7
Intervention Board for Agricultural Produce, 71
objects of Communities considered in relation to, 30, 30.3
powers to make, 13, 30, 30.7, 30.10
procedure for, 30.5
provisions as to, 58
restrictive trade practices, in relation to, 38, 38.7
scope of, 30.10
SUGAR,
amendments to law, 2, 32.1, 33.14, 60
Commonwealth Sugar Agreement, 35.1
determination of prices, 35, 35.3
phased substitution of Community law, 31.7, 32.1, 35, 35.1–35.4
SUGAR BOARD,
financing, 30.8
levies, 30.9, 35, 35.1, 35.2, 35.3

TAXATION,
powers to make provision relating to, 30.3, 57
value added tax. *See* VALUE ADDED TAX
TREATIES. *See also* COMMUNITY LAW
decisions on and proof of, 29, 31
definition of, 29
direct effects of, within a member state, 9, 10
directly applicable, 16–22, 30.1
enforcement of, 1, 2, 28, 28.1, 28.2, 29, 30, 30.2, 30.3
See also implementation, *below*
European Court, powers given to, 31, 31.1
implementation of—
by regulations, 29, 30, 30.10
Channel Islands, in, 30, 30.11
commencement, 30.1
Gibraltar, in, 30, 30.11
Isle of Man, in, 30, 30.11
Northern Ireland, in, 29, 30, 30.10
payments, community obligation to make, 30, 30.7–30.9
provisions, 1, 2, 30, 30.1, 30.3
See also enforcement, *above*
TREATIES—*continued*
indirect effects of, within a member state, 9, 10
interpretation of by European Court, 31, 31.2
judicial notice to be taken of, 29, 31, 31.4
legal effect of, 30, 30.1
made after 22nd January 1972, position of U.K. in relation to, 29, 29.1, 29.2, 29.3
novelty of original three, 3–8
obligations under, 30, 30.1
pre-accession, 29, 29.1, 29.2, 41–47
primary source of Communities law, 29.1
procedures provided for, by or under, 30, 30.1
question as to meaning or effect of, treated as question of law, 31, 31.1
remedies provided for, by or under, 30, 30.1
TREATY,
definition of, for purposes of s. 1 (2), (3), 29, 29.4
TREATY OF ACCESSION,
according U.K. entry to Communities, 11, 29, 29.1, 29.2
entry date, 54
provisions relating to position of—
Channel Islands, 28.1
Gibraltar, 28.2
Isle of Man, 28.1
TREATY OF BRUSSELS. *See* TREATY OF ACCESSION
TREATY OF LUXEMBOURG,
definition of, 46

UNITED KINGDOM,
accession of, to—
European Atomic Energy Community, treaty relating to, 29
European Coal and Steel Community, decision relating to, 29
European Economic Community. *See* TREATY OF ACCESSION
amendments to law of, by reason of Community obligations, 1, 2, 31.7 32, 32.1
autonomous legal order, an, 11–15
Community law—
application of, 1–27, 31, 31.1–31.6
evidence in, 31, 31.4–31.6
inclusion of, in European Communities, 28, 28.1, 28.2
legislation, impact of Act on, 3–8, 23–27
obligations of, implementation of, 30.3
payments by, to Communities, 30, 30.7
rights of, 30.3, 30.6
UNITS OF MEASUREMENT, 30.3

VALUE ADDED TAX,
Gibraltar, position of, in relation to, 28.2
implementation of, 2, 30.3
payment out of, to Communities, 30.7

All references are to paragraph numbers